Authentic Narrative of the Death of Lord Nelson

by

William Beatty

Comments and Supplementary Material

by

AJ Noon

Front Cover Image: Admiral Nelson, before Trafalgar (by Charles Lucy, 1854), Rijksmuseum RP-P-OB-73.047

Publishing Information

1st Published April 2024

All rights reserved. No part of this publication may be reproduced, stored in a retrieval system, or transmitted in any form or by any means, electronic, mechanical, photocopying, recording, or otherwise, without the prior permission of both the copyright owners and the below publisher of this book.

Version 1.20

www.redvarkpublishing.co.uk

redvarkpub@gmail.com *@redvarkpub*

A ridiculous amount of thanks (as always) to KSL for her hard work

Scans from my own collection unless otherwise noted

Table of Contents

Introduction 5

A Biography of William Beatty 7

The Battle of Trafalgar – The Buildup 11

AUTHENTIC NARRATIVE OF THE DEATH OF LORD NELSON 14

The Death of Nelson by Arthur William Devis, 1807 60

The Battle of Trafalgar – The Aftermath 62

Changing Spaces 64

A Surgeon's Toolkit 69

A Surgeon's Medicines 71

Treatments 73

Things to See 82

Further Reading and Resources 84

A Drop of Nelson's Blood 87

Index 92

The Battle of Trafalgar, 1805 (after Paul Léon Jazet), Rijksmuseum RP-P-2018-536

Take a tour through the iconic ship that is arguably Portsmouth's most famous landmark, HMS *Victory*.

This book guides you deck-by-deck through the ship, bringing to life the wooden walls and the lives of the sailors who were on her.

Written by local author and guide AJ Noon, for every copy sold a donation is made to the *National Museum of the Royal Navy*, who look after the ship.

The Essential Visual HMS Victory

AJ Noon

Introduction

In 1807, Sir William Beatty published his account of the death of Vice-Admiral Lord Horatio Nelson, who died on the 21st of October, 1805, at the Battle of Trafalgar. Beatty was the surgeon onboard HMS *Victory*, Nelson's flagship, and not only attended Nelson as he died, but also performed the autopsy on the body. Actually two autopsies; a simple one the day after the battle and a more complete one on the 12th of December, where he extracted the musket-ball that killed Nelson.

His account, which also includes details of the battle and the events leading up to it, has been published many times since. Usually printed as a standalone volume, there is little included to bring to life Beatty, the experiences of a naval surgeon, or details of a surgeon's skills (it's 1805, surgeons are quite skilled by then!).

With this book I present to you Beatty's account of the death of Nelson and supplementary material that I hope gives you a better insight into the period. Though I have tidied up the original text and moved the footnotes from his appendix to the relevant pages, I have not changed the language – so read *'chace'* as *'chase'*, and some of the names listed by Beatty are known differently now, such as *'Dumanoir'* for *'Dumannoir'*. I have also added extra illustrations, the only one in the original publication was that of the musket-ball.

I have added my own footnotes as well, and these are in bold to differentiate them from the original text.

AJ Noon

We are a small independent publisher, and reviews mean everything to us. The world of books is ruled by algorithms and the visibility of this book, and our others, relies on you the reader leaving a review. You have given us your precious time to read this book, which we already greatly appreciate, but if we could ask you to leave an honest review on the review site of your choice (Amazon, LibraryThing, Book Riot, Booklist, LoveReading, Goodreads, etc), then you have our gratitude.

Your reviews also help shape our future books as we get a better idea of what our readers like and want more of.

Redvark Publishing Limited

THE MAN WHO TENDED NELSON AT HIS LAST HOUR: SIR WILLIAM BEATTY, THE SURGEON IN THE "VICTORY" AT TRAFALGAR, WRITER OF THE "NARRATIVE OF THE DEATH OF LORD NELSON."

A Biography of William Beatty

William Beatty was born in April 1773 in Londonderry, Ireland, the eldest of six children. Several of his family members, including his father, were excisemen, but it is likely that his uncle on his mother's side, naval surgeon George Smyth, was the inspiration for his career choice. In 1791 an eighteen-year-old Beatty presented himself before the London Company of Surgeons to be tested, and within a week was assigned as surgeon's second mate on HMS *Dictator*[1] (which was being re-commissioned, and would not sail until January 1793[2]).

Within four months Beatty was re-assigned to HMS *Iphigenia*[3], and achieved promotion to first mate in February 1793 with a move to HMS *Hermione*[4]. At the end of the year, the schooner *Flying Fish*[5] lost her surgeon and Beatty was appointed acting surgeon. Working heavily in the West Indies at this time, Beatty would have experienced the diseases of the locality, especially yellow fever.

In the June of 1794, Beatty was transferred to HMS *Alligator*, which became badly hit by yellow fever. On the ship's return to England in 1795, he once again presented himself before the London Company of Surgeons, and this time was rated as a surgeon for a second-rate[6].

Just as his star was rising, Captain Augustus Fitzroy of his next ship, HMS *Pomona*, had Beatty brought up on charges of contempt as they argued about the fitness of some of the sick sailors. Beatty was confined for two weeks before the courts-

---

[1] A third-rate of 64 guns, launched originally in 1783, and was paid off in 1815.

[2] Ships have many dates attached to them: Ordered, laid down (when construction started), Launched, Commissioned, Paid Off, Re-Commissioned, and Sold/Scrapped. In this book I have listed the launch dates of ships, as that gives a better idea of the age of them, especially if you look at HMS *Victory*, which was ordered in 1758, laid down in 1759, launched in 1765, but was not commissioned (saw service) until 1778.

[3] An *Amazon* class fifth-rate of 38 guns, launched in 1780 which caught fire (accidentally) and was destroyed in 1801 in Aboukir Bay.

[4] Launched in 1782, a fifth-rate of 38 guns. In 1797, the crew mutinied and delivered the ship to the Spanish. The British recaptured her in 1799, and renamed her HMS *Retaliation*. She was renamed again to *Retribution*, before being broken up in 1805.

[5] Originally the French schooner *L'Esperanza*, carrying 4 guns.

[6] Warships at the time were rated by the number of guns they carried, so a first-rate was 100+ guns, a second-rate 90-98 guns, a third-rate 64-84 guns. The schooner Flying Fish was unrated, carrying just 6 guns.

martial onboard HMS Malabar on August the 4th. He was cleared at the trial, and the board commented that they found Fitzroy's charges were frivolous.

They only had to work together for another month after this event, and Beatty moved to HMS *Amethyst*[7], serving under Captain Thomas Affleck (who he had served under on HMS *Alligator*). This ship was wrecked on rocks off Alderney in December, and Beatty would find himself onboard HMS *Alcmene* next.

He served on her from March 1796 through to March 1801, as she primarily patrolled the eastern Atlantic and escorted convoys to and from Portugal. The Alcmene joined Nelson's fleets shortly after the Battle of the Nile, and was with him at Naples in January 1799 when they evacuated the Neapolitan royal family. In October of that year, Captain Henry Digby took command of the ship[8], and he proved to be a particularly aggressive (to the enemy) and successful captain. In around fifteen months they had captured as many ships, which not only helped to enrich Beatty, it also gave him much opportunity to practice his surgeons skills as he tended to the wounded in each instance.

When Digby moved to HMS *Resistance*[9] at the start of 1801, Beatty went with him, serving until January the following year, when the Treaty of Amiens meant the Royal Navy did not need as many active ships. Peace was short-lived, and Beatty signed to HMS *Spencer* in the July 0f 1803, but this ship struck rocks off Ferrol in 1804 and returned to Plymouth for repairs.

It is at that juncture Beatty and Nelson finally served together (though they may have met at Naples, and possibly even Aboukir Bay) with Beatty joining HMS *Victory*[10] in the December of 1804. The following year was the fateful Battle of Trafalgar, at which Beatty performed eleven amputations. If you have visited the cockpit on HMS *Victory*, or looked at the photos further into this book, you can barely imagine what it must have been like down there during battle. Dimly lit, low headroom, the largest guns firing on the deck above you, and the injured and dying filling the spaces around you; it would have been an intense time for the surgeon and his assistants.

---

[7] **Originally the French ship *Perle*, surrendered to the Royal Navy in 1793 at Toulon. She was a *Junon* class fifth-rate launched in 1790, and was wrecked off Alderney in 1795.**

[8] **He would captain HMS *Africa* at the Battle of Trafalgar.**

[9] **A 36-gun *Aigle* class fifth-rate, launched in 1801, wrecked near Cape St. Vincent in 1803.**

[10] **A 104-gun first rate, launched in 1765 (though originally launched with 100 guns). She is now a museum ship in Portsmouth, England.**

After Trafalgar, HMS *Victory* returned to England, and following Nelson's funeral on January the 9th, 1806, Beatty transferred to HMS *Sussex*, a hospital ship that was moored near Sheerness. The subsequent year he left that ship, and also had his account of Nelson's death published. In part, he published his account because others who had served on *Victory* were selling their own versions of Nelson's last moments to the newspapers, and Beatty had also received criticism from some quarters for using brandy and not rum to preserve the body – this was his opportunity to set the record straight and to defend his choices.

In September, 1807, he became physician of the Channel Fleet which he served in two stints up until August 1815. With peace returning to Europe after the defeat of Napoleon, the Royal Navy once again wound down the numbers of ships it required to be active. Beatty was a civilian once more (though still subject to being called-up by the Royal Navy if war broke out again).

Beatty spent two years studying in Edinburgh, before opening his own practice in Plymouth in 1810. In 1822, he returned to London where he became the physician for Greenwich Hospital (a naval, though land-based, post). In 1824 he became a director of the Clerical, Medical and General Life Assurance Company (now known as Clerical Medical), and then also of the London and Greenwich Railway.

In the March of 1838, during his last years at Greenwich, Beatty joined the project to build Nelson's Column, led by the Duke of Wellington, had begun. Shortly after his retirement in October 1839, it was erroneously reported by The Times newspaper that he had died, forcing them to publish a retraction two days later.

Unfortunately, he did not live to see Trafalgar Square finished, or even the statue raised atop the column, as he died on the 25th of March, 1842[11]. He was interred in an unmarked vault at Kensal Green cemetery, London. He never married and had no children.

---

[11] **The statue of Nelson was positioned in November 1843. The last of the four bronze plaques around the base was placed in 1853, and the lions were added in 1867.**

Ship Name	Size	From	To	Captain
HMS *Dictator*	64-gun third-rate	May 1791	September 1791	Thomas Tonken
HMS *Iphigenia*	32-gun fifth-rate frigate	September 1791	February 1793	Patrick Sinclair
HMS *Hermione*	32-gun fifth-rate frigate	February 1793	December 1793	John Hills
HMS *Flying Fish*	6-gun unrated schooner	December 1793	June 1794	James Prevost
HMS *Alligator*	26-gun sixth-rate frigate	June 1794	February 1795	Thomas Surridge
HMS *Pomona*[12]	28-gun sixth-rate frigate	March 1795	September 1795	Augustus Fitzroy
HMS *Amethyst*	36-gun fifth-rate frigate	September 1795	December 1795	Thomas Affleck
HMS *Alcmene*	32-gun fifth-rate frigate	March 1795	May 1801	Henry Digby
HMS *Resistance*	36-gun fifth-rate	May 1801	January 1802	Henry Digby
HMS *Spencer*	74-gun third-rate	July 1803	December 1804	Robert Stopford
HMS *Victory*	104-gun first-rate	December 1804	January 1806	Thomas Hardy Flagship of Horatio Nelson
HMS *Sussex*[13]	Hospital ship	February 1806	September 1806	Richard Jewers
Physician of the Channel Fleet		September 1806	August 1815[14]	
Physician to Greenwich Hospital		September 1822	July 1839	

---

[12] **Re-named HMS *Amphitrite* in 1794**

[13] **Originally HMS *Union*, a 90-gun second-rate.**

[14] **He was released in October 1914, then re-appointed in May 1815.**

The Battle of Trafalgar – The Buildup

As dawn broke on the 21st of October, 1805, many of the crew of the British ships assembled off the coast of Spain cheered at the sight in front of them. In the distance were the masts of the Combined Fleets; eighteen French ships and fifteen Spanish ships (and seven French support vessels), under the command of Admiral Villeneuve. But this was no chance meeting, for the British fleet - numbering twenty-seven ships with six support vessels) - under Vice-Admiral Horatio Nelson, had been harrying this fleet for over seven months, trying to force the fight.

At the start of 1805, Nelson and his fleet had been keeping Admiral Villeneuve contained in Toulon, France, by blockading to stop the enemy from sailing out. This was a tactic the Royal Navy were using across the ports used by the French, and a considerable proportion of the Royal Navy was dedicated to blockade duties.

Towards the end of March, Nelson drew the twelve ships under his command back from the immediate vicinity of Toulon, both to re-supply and in the hope of luring Villeneuve and his eleven ships out to battle. Villeneuve put to sea on March 30th, but he learnt of the location of Nelson's ships and, with assistance from the weather, avoided Nelson completely.

Nelson learnt of Villeneuve leaving Toulon, but did not know of their destination, so he took a gamble that they would be heading towards Egypt and started sailing in that direction. Villeneuve, however, left the Mediterranean, picking up extra ships from Cadiz and headed to the West Indies. Six Spanish ships, under the command of Gravina, followed to catch up with him.

Nelson realised that Villeneuve had left the Mediterranean, but again he did not know which way the French Admiral would go but made the assumption that it would be towards the West Indies as the British had valuable trade routes there and a French fleet loose in the area would cause havoc to the trade and supply lines. Nelson had guessed correctly but was now a month behind the French. Remember that this was the age-of-sail, so sailing speed and course was completely dictated by the wind direction.

Villeneuve arrived in Martinique on the 14th of May, where he was joined by Admiral Gravina[15], and they spent the following weeks attacking British interests in the area. On June the 7th, near Antigua, Villeneuve captured a convoy of British merchants, and from them learnt that Nelson had arrived at Barbados just three days prior. It was at this point he decided to head back to Europe, so he began the long voyage back across the Atlantic with Nelson following – they passed Antigua within a day of each other.

---

[15] **Don Federico Carlos Gravina (1756 – 1806)**

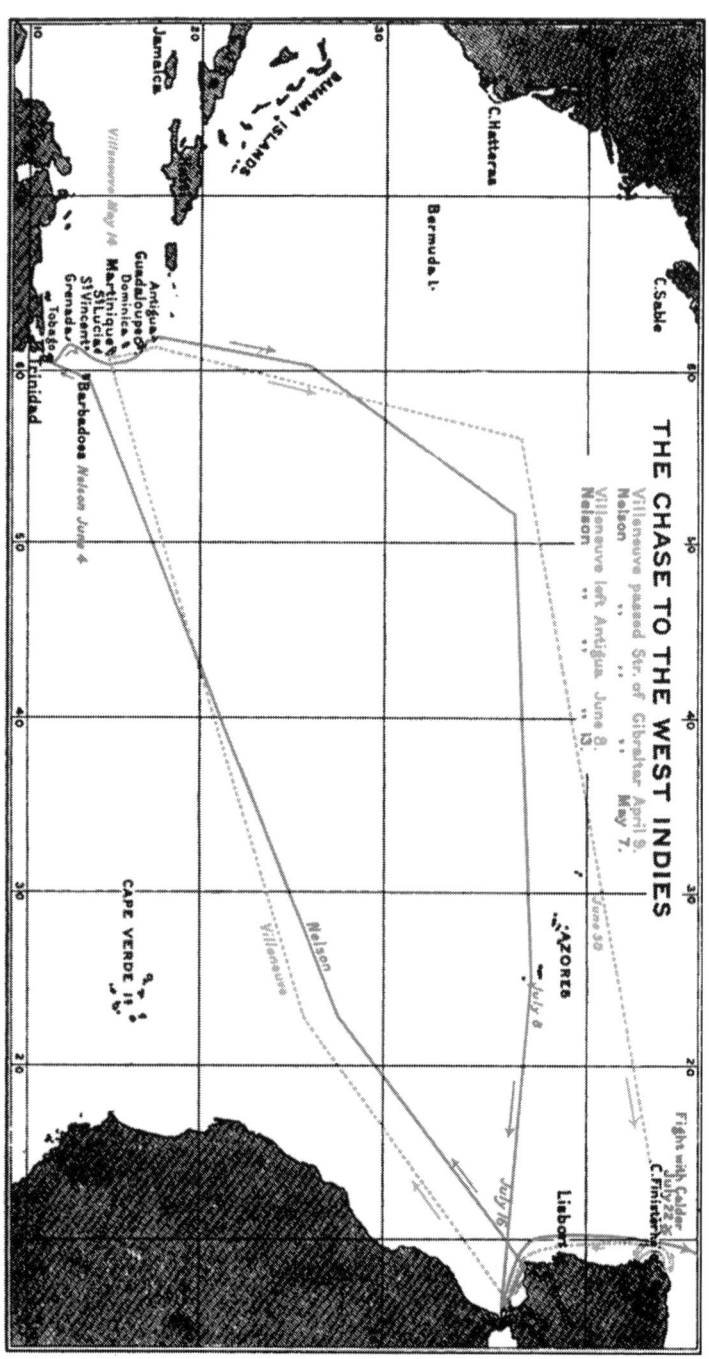

Again, not knowing the route Villeneuve was taking, Nelson headed towards Gibraltar, sailing too far south of the Combined Fleets, but they were intercepted by Robert Calder and his fleet off Cape Finisterre, on the 22nd of July. At this point, the Combined Fleets numbered twenty ships and seven support vessels (frigates), whilst the British numbered fifteen ships with four support vessels. The action started late in the afternoon with poor visibility, and by nightfall two of the Spanish ships were captured (*San Rafael* of 80 guns and *Firme* of 74 guns).

The following morning the two fleets were still in sight of each other, but neither attacked - for which Robert Calder would be summoned back to England in October to answer for not pressing the attack, thus missing the Battle of Trafalgar. Admiral Villeneuve took his fleet back to Cadiz, arriving there in the middle of August. Here they would remain, until setting sail again on October 20th, where they were sighted by the frigates Nelson had tasked with watching Cadiz.

For nearly seven months, Nelson had chased Villeneuve from the Mediterranean, to the West Indies, and back, so now the sailing was finally over, and it was time for the men to prove their mettle.

Fleets of the time were not a fixed number, as you can see from above where the number in the Combined Fleets changes. If Villeneuve had sailed from Cadiz a fortnight earlier then the British would have thirty-three or thirty-four ships for the fight rather than twenty-seven, as six had been sent to resupply and Robert Calder (in the 98 gun *HMS Prince of Wales*) had returned to England to explain his actions at Cape Finisterre.

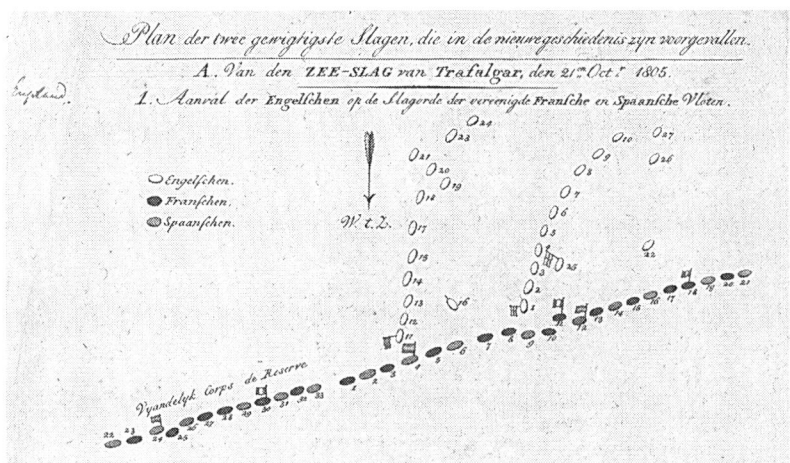

Order of Battle, courtesy of the Rijksmuseum, RP-P-2018-534

AUTHENTIC NARRATIVE OF THE DEATH OF LORD NELSON

WITH

THE CIRCUMSTANCES PRECEDING, ATTENDING, AND

SUBSEQUENT TO, THAT EVENT;

THE PROFESSIONAL REPORT

ON HIS LORDSHIP'S WOUND,

AND SEVERAL INTERESTING ANECDOTES.

BY WILLIAM BEATTY, M.D.

Surgeon to the Victory in the Battle of Trafalgar,

and now Physician to the Fleet under the Command

of the Earl of St. Vincent, K.B. &c. &c. &c.

LONDON:

PRINTED BY T. DAVISON, WHITE-FRIARS;

FOR T. CADELL AND W. DAVIES, IN THE STRAND.

1807.

TO THE PUBLIC.

The Surgeon of the late illustrious Lord NELSON feels himself called upon, from the responsible situation which he held on the eventful day of the 21st of October 1805, to lay before the British Nation the following Narrative. It contains an account of the most interesting incidents which occurred on board the Victory, (Lord NELSON's flag-ship) from the time of her sailing from England, in the month of September, till the day of battle inclusively; with a detail of the particulars of HIS LORDSHIP'S Death, the mode adopted for preserving his revered Remains during the subsequent long passage of the Victory to England, and the condition of the Body when it was deposited in Greenwich Hospital[16]. This short statement of facts is deemed a small but necessary tribute of respect to the memory of the departed Hero, as well as a professional document which the Public had a right to expect from the man who had the melancholy honour of being his principal medical attendant on that occasion: and is presumed to be not unappropriately concluded by observations on the state of HIS LORDSHIP'S health for some time previous to his fall; with his habits of life, and other circumstances, strongly proving that few men had a greater prospect of attaining longevity, on which account his premature death is the more to be deplored by his Country.

GREENWICH HOSPITAL.

---

[16] Greenwich Hospital was a retirement home for old sailors, opening in 1692 and closing in 1869. Christopher Wren and Nicholas Hawksmoor designed the original buildings, and the Painted Hall is where Nelson's body was laid in state. Some of the buildings are now used by the University of Greenwich and other organisations.

It was originally intended that this Narrative should be published in the LIFE OF LORD NELSON, undertaken by the Rev. J.S. CLARKE and J. M'ARTHUR, Esq. and it will still form a part of that Work; but from the length of time which must necessarily elapse before so extensive and magnificent a Publication can be completed, the Author has been induced to print it in a separate form.

Narrative

Lord NELSON sailed from St. Helen's[17] in the Victory, with the Euryalus frigate, on the morning of the 15th of September 1805, to take the command of the British Fleet cruizing before Cadiz. On the 18th he appeared off Plymouth; where he was joined by his Majesty's ships Thunderer and Ajax, with which he proceeded for his destined station. On the 20th he communicated by private signal with the squadron under the command of Rear-Admiral STIRLING[18], which passed within a few miles of the Victory; and the same day at noon, spoke his Majesty's ship Le Decade[19], having on board Rear-Admiral Sir RICHARD BICKERTON[20], who, was on his return to England for the recovery of his health.

CUTHBERT, LORD COLLINGWOOD

Some bad weather and adverse winds were experienced by the Victory in crossing the Bay of Biscay, and on the 27th Cape St. Vincent[21] was seen. Lord NELSON had dispatched the Euryalus ahead on the preceding day, to acquaint Admiral COLLINGWOOD[22] with his approach; and to direct that no salute should take place, nor any public compliments be paid to his flag, on his assuming

---

[17] On the east coast of the Isle of Wight.
[18] Eventually Vice-Admiral Charles Stirling (1760-1833).
[19] *Décade* was a Galathée-class French frigate launched in 1794 and captured on August 24th, 1798, by HMS *Naiad* under the command of Captain William Pierrepoint (1766-1813).
[20] Eventually Admiral Richard Bickerton (1759-1832).
[21] Cabo de Sao Vicente, the south-west tip of Portugal.
[22] Eventually Vice-Admiral Cuthbert Collingwood (1748 – 1810).

the command, as he wished the Enemy to be kept ignorant of a reinforcement being received by the British Fleet. In the evening of the 28th, the Victory joined the Fleet; now consisting of twenty-seven ships of the line, including the Victory, Ajax, and Thunderer: the city of Cadiz was seen distant about fifteen miles, with the Combined Fleets at anchor; and Admiral LOUIS[23], with five or six ships under his command, close in shore, watching the motions of the Enemy.

On the 29th, prompt and decisive measures were adopted to prevent the Enemy from receiving any supplies of provisions by sea, which His LORDSHIP was informed they were very much distressed for: cruisers were stationed off the Capes St. Vincent, St. Mary's, and Trafalgar; and the frigates Euryalus and Hydra were ordered to keep off the entrance of Cadiz. His LORDSHIP now retired with the Fleet to the vicinity of Cape St. Mary's[24], about fifty or sixty miles westward of Cadiz; keeping up a constant communication with the frigates in shore, by means of three or four ships of the line placed at convenient intervals for distinguishing the signals of each other. This distance from, the Enemy's port was preserved by His LORDSHIP, to prevent them from being speedily acquainted with the force of the Fleet under his command; and that he might avoid the necessity of bearing up in bad weather, and running with the Fleet through the Straits of Gibraltar when the westerly gales prevailed: as the inconvenience of being forced into the Mediterranean, had been felt by former Commanders in Chief; and would now have afforded a favourable opportunity to the Enemy of effecting their escape from Cadiz, or at all events have rendered their obtaining supplies less difficult.

On the 1st of October Admiral LOUIS joined the Fleet, with a part of his squadron (the Canopus, Spencer, and Tigre), from before Cadiz; and departed the next day with those ships, the Queen, and the Zealous, for Gibraltar[25], to procure a supply of provisions, stores, and water, which they were much in want of. On the 4th he rejoined with his squadron; having received intelligence from the Euryalus by telegraph, that the French ships in Cadiz were embarking their troops, and preparing to sail. Lord NELSON however conceived this to be merely intended as a stratagem, to draw him nearer to Cadiz, for the purpose of obtaining a knowledge of his force; and therefore directed Admiral LOUIS to proceed in the execution of the orders before delivered to him.

---

[23] **Eventually Rear-Admiral Thomas Louis (1757 – 1807).**

[24] **Cabo de Santa Maria, the southernmost tip of Portugal.**

[25] **Gibraltar was captured by the English in 1704 and possession ceded by the Spanish in the 1713 Treaty of Utrecht.**

Between the 7th and the 13th, His LORDSHIP was reinforced by the Royal Sovereign, Belleisle, Defiance, Agamemnon, and Africa, from England, and the Leviathan from Gibraltar. The Agamemnon, Sir EDWARD BERRY[26], joined on the 13th;[27] with intelligence that she had been chased on the coast of Portugal a few days before by an Enemy's squadron, consisting of six sail of the line.

On the 13th in the evening, Sir ROBERT CALDER[28], in his Majesty's ship the Prince of Wales, parted company with the Fleet, on his return to England. His departure Lord NELSON had some days before evinced an anxious wish to procrastinate, and was heard that very day to declare his firm belief that the Combined Fleets would be at sea in the course of ten days or a fortnight.[29]

On the 18th the Donegal, Captain MALCOLM, left the Fleet for Gibraltar. On the 19th his Majesty's ships the Colossus, Mars, Defence, and Agamemnon, formed the cordon of communication with the frigates in shore: the Fleet was lying to. About half past nine in the morning, the Mars, being one of the ships nearest to the Fleet, repeated the signal from the ships further in shore, that "*the Enemy were coming out of port.*" Lord NELSON immediately ordered the general signal to be made, with two guns, for a chace in the south-east quarter. The wind was now very light;

---

[26] **Eventually Rear-Admiral Edward Berry (1768 – 1831).**

[27] By this ship His LORDSHIP received some newspapers from England, one of which contained a paragraph stating that General MACK was about to be appointed to the command of the Austrian armies in Germany. On reading this, His LORDSHIP made the following observation: "*I know General MACK too well. He sold the King of Naples; and if he is now entrusted with an important command, he will certainly betray the Austrian monarchy.*"

[28] **Eventually Admiral Robert Calder (1745 – 1818). After the Battle of Cape Finisterre, where he intercepted the Combined Fleets, he was summoned back to England for a courts-martial for not pressing the attack. He was acquitted but missed the Battle of Trafalgar.**

[29] CAPTAIN HARDY left England in a bad state of health, with which he had been afflicted during the last twelve months; but was now in a progressive state of amendment. Lord NELSON asked the Surgeon this day, "*how long he thought it might be before Captain HARDY'S perfect recovery;*" and on the Surgeon's answering that "*he hoped not more than a fortnight,*"—"*Ah!*" replied His LORDSHIP, "*before a fortnight the Enemy will be at sea, the business will be done, and we shall be looking out for England.*"

[30] **Eventually Admiral Pulteney Malcolm (1768 – 1838).**

and the breezes partial, mostly from the south-south-west. The Fleet made all possible sail; and about two o'clock the Colossus and Mars repeated signals from the ships in shore, communicating the welcome intelligence of "*the Enemy being at sea.*" This cheered the minds of all on board, with the prospect of realizing those hopes of meeting the Enemy which had been so long and so sanguinely entertained. It was well known to His LORDSHIP, that all the Enemy's ships had the iron hoops on their masts painted black; whereas the British ships, with the exception of the Belleisle and Polyphemus, had theirs painted yellow: and as he considered that this would serve for a very good mark of distinction in the heat of battle, he made known this circumstance to the Fleet, and ordered the Belleisle and Polyphemus to paint their hoops yellow; but the evening being far advanced when the signal was made to them for this purpose, His LORDSHIP, fearing that it might not be distinctly understood, sent the Entreprenante cutter to them to communicate the order.

During the night the Fleet continued steering to the south-east under all sail, in expectation of seeing the Enemy; and at day-break on the 20th found itself in the entrance of the Straits of Gibraltar, but nothing of the Enemy to be discovered. The Fleet now wore, and made sail to the north-west; and at seven in the morning the Phoebe was seen making signals for "*the Enemy bearing north.*" At eight o'clock the Victory hove to; and Admiral COLLINGWOOD, with the Captains of the Mars, Colossus, and Defence,[31] came on board, to receive instructions from His LORDSHIP; at eleven minutes past nine they returned to their respective ships, and the Fleet made sail again to the northward.

In the afternoon the wind increased, and blew fresh from the south-west; which excited much apprehension on board the Victory, lest the Enemy might be forced to return to port. The look-out ships, however, made several signals for seeing them, and to report their force and bearings. His LORDSHIP was at this time on the poop; and turning round, and observing a group of Midshipmen assembled together, he said to them with a smile, "*This day or to-morrow will be a fortunate one for you, young men,*" alluding to their being promoted in the event of a victory.

---

[31] **Captain George Duff (1764 – 1805, killed at Trafalgar) of HMS *Mars*, Captain James Nicoll Morris (1763 – 1830) of HMS *Colossus*, Captain George Hope (1767 – 1818) of HMS *Defence*.**

A little before sunset the Euryalus communicated intelligence by telegraph, that "*the Enemy appeared determined to go to the westward.*" His LORDSHIP upon this ordered it to be signified to Captain BLACKWOOD[32] (of that ship) by signal, that "*he depended on the Euryalus[33] for keeping sight of the Enemy during the night.*" The night signals were so clearly and distinctly arranged by His LORDSHIP, and so well understood by the respective Captains, that the Enemy's motions continued to be made known to him with the greatest facility throughout the night: a certain number of guns, with false fires and blue lights announced their altering their course, wearing, and making or shortening sail; and signals communicating such changes were repeated by the look-out ships, from the Euryalus to the Victory.

The Enemy wore twice during the night: which evolution was considered by His LORDSHIP as shewing an intention, on their part, of keeping the port of Cadiz open; and made him apprehend that on seeing the British Fleet, they would effect their retreat thither before he could bring them to a general action. He was therefore very careful not to approach their Fleet near enough to be seen by them before morning.

The British Fleet wore about two o'clock in the morning; and stood on the larboard tack with their heads to the northward, carrying their topsails and foresails, and anxiously expecting the dawn of day. When that period arrived, the Combined Fleets were distinctly seen from the Victory's deck, formed in a close line of battle ahead on the starboard tack, standing to the south, and about twelve miles to leeward. They consisted of thirty-three ships of the line; four of which were three-deckers, and one of seventy guns: the strength of the British Fleet was twenty-seven ships of the line; seven of which were three-deckers, and three of sixty-four guns. Lord NELSON had, on the 10th, issued written Instructions to the Admirals and Captains of the Fleet individually, pointing out his intended mode of attack in the event of meeting the Enemy;[34] and now, previously to appearing himself on deck, he directed Captain HARDY to make the necessary signals for the order and disposition of the Fleet accordingly.

---

[32] **Eventually Vice-Admiral Henry Blackwood (1770 – 1832).**

[33] **HMS *Euryalus* was an Apollo-class frigate, built at Buckler's Hard, Hampshire, and launched in 1803.**

[34] These Instructions will be found at the end of the Narrative.

HIS LORDSHIP came upon deck soon after day-light: he was dressed as usual in his Admiral's frock-coat, bearing on the left breast four stars of different orders which he always wore with his common apparel.[35] He displayed excellent spirits, and expressed his pleasure at the prospect of giving a fatal blow to the naval power of France and Spain; and spoke with confidence of obtaining a signal victory notwithstanding the inferiority of the British Fleet, declaring to Captain HARDY that "*he would not be contented with capturing less than twenty sail of the line.*" He afterwards pleasantly observed that "*the 21st of October was the happiest day in the year among his family,*" but did not assign the reason of this.[36] His LORDSHIP had previously entertained a strong presentiment that this would prove the auspicious day; and had several times said to Captain HARDY and Doctor SCOTT[37] (Chaplain of the ship, and Foreign Secretary to the Commander in Chief, whose intimate friendship he enjoyed), "*The 21st of October will be our day.*"

The wind was now from the west; but the breezes were very light, with a long heavy swell running. The signal being made for bearing down upon the Enemy in two lines, the British Fleet set all possible sail. The lee line, consisting of thirteen ships, was led by Admiral COLLINGWOOD in the Royal Sovereign; and the weather line, composed of fourteen ships, by the Commander in Chief in the Victory. HIS LORDSHIP had ascended the poop, to have a better view of both lines of the British Fleet; and while there, gave particular directions for taking down from his cabin the different fixtures, and for being very careful in removing the portrait of Lady HAMILTON[38]: "*Take care of my Guardian Angel,*" said he, addressing himself to the

---

[35] HIS LORDSHIP did not wear his sword in the Battle of Trafalgar: it had been taken from the place where it hung up in his cabin, and was laid ready on his table; but it is supposed he forgot to call for it. This was the only action in which he ever appeared without a sword.

[36] It has been since recollected that on the 21st of October 1757, His LORDSHIP'S maternal uncle, Captain SUCKLING, in the Dreadnought, in company with two other line of battle ships, attacked and beat off a French squadron of four sail of the line and three frigates, off Cape François. The French Commodore was towed into Cape François; and the English ships, being too much disabled to follow up their success, bore away to Jamaica to refit.

[37] **Alexander John Scott (1768 – 1840). Nelson had Scott transferred to *Victory* in 1804 as he had seen him at work drawing up the treaties after the Battle of Copenhagen (1801). He was not a doctor at the time but Nelson called him Dr Scott to differentiate him from his secretary, John Scott.**

[38] **Born Amy Lyon in Cheshire in 1765, she died in 1815 in Calais, France. She first met Nelson in Naples 1793, but it was when he returned after the Battle of the Nile in 1798 that their affair began. Nelson was married to Frances Nisbet (nee Woolward) in 1787, though they had no children from the union.**

persons to be employed in this business. Immediately after this he quitted the poop, and retired to his cabin for a few minutes: where he committed to paper the following short but devout and fervent ejaculation, which must be universally admired as truly characteristic of the Christian hero; and the codicil to his will, which follows it:

> MAY the great GOD whom I worship grant to my Country, and for the benefit of Europe in general, a great and glorious victory; and may no misconduct in any one tarnish it, and may humanity after victory be the predominant feature in the British Fleet! For myself individually, I commit my life to Him that made me; and may His blessing alight on my endeavours for serving my Country faithfully! To Him I resign myself, and the just cause which is entrusted to me to defend. Amen, Amen, Amen.

> OCTOBER 21st, 1805. Then in sight of the Combined Fleets of France and Spain, distant about ten miles.

> WHEREAS the eminent services of EMMA HAMILTON, widow of the Right Honourable Sir WILLIAM HAMILTON[39], have been of the very greatest service to my King and Country, to my knowledge, without ever receiving any reward from either our King or Country:

> First, that she obtained the King of Spain's letter, in 1796, to his brother the King of Naples[40], acquainting him of his intention to declare war against England; from which letter the ministry sent out orders to the then Sir JOHN JERVIS[41], to strike a stroke if opportunity offered, against either the arsenals of Spain or her fleets:—that neither of these was done, is not the fault of Lady HAMILTON; the opportunity might have been offered:[42]

> Secondly: the British Fleet under my command could never have returned the second time to Egypt, had not Lady HAMILTON'S influence with the

---

[39] **William Hamilton (1730 – 1803).**

[40] **Ferdinand I of the Two Sicilies (1751 – 1825).**

[41] **Eventually Admiral of the Fleet John Jervis (1735 – 1823).**

[42] This phrase has been subjected to misconstruction; to the Writer of these pages, however, both the purport and expression of it seem very clear, thus; "*might have been offered*" (though it was not).

Queen of Naples[43] caused letters to be wrote to the Governor of Syracuse, that he was to encourage the Fleet's being supplied with every thing, should they put into any port in Sicily. We put into Syracuse[44], and received every supply; went to Egypt, and destroyed the French Fleet:

Could I have rewarded these services, I would not now call upon my Country; but as that has not been in my power, I leave EMMA Lady HAMILTON therefore a legacy to my King and Country, that they will give her an ample provision to maintain her rank in life.

I also leave to the beneficence of my Country my adopted Daughter, HORATIA NELSON THOMPSON; and I desire she will use in future the name of NELSON only.

These are the only favours I ask of my King and Country, at this moment when I am going to fight their battle. May GOD bless my King and Country, and all those I hold dear! My Relations it is needless to mention: they will of course be amply provided for.

NELSON and BRONTE[45].

Witness HENRY BLACKWOOD T.M. Hardy

The prayer and codicil were both written with HIS LORDSHIP'S own hand, within three hours before the commencement of the engagement.

As the Victory drew near to the Enemy, HIS LORDSHIP, accompanied by Captain HARDY[46], and the Captains of the four frigates (Euryalus, Naiad, Sirius, and Phoebe)[47] who had been called on board by signal to receive instructions, visited the different decks of the ship. He addressed the crew at their several quarters,

---

[43] Maria Carolina (1752 – 1814), Queen of Naples and Sicily

[44] South-eastern Sicily.

[45] Nelson assisted King Ferdinand I of the Two Sicilies in Naples in 1799, and was rewarded with the title *Duke of Bronte*, leading to his signature from this point of *Nelson and Bronte*.

[46] Eventually Vice-Admiral Thomas Masterman Hardy (1769 – 1839).

[47] Captain Henry Blackwood (1770 - 1832) of HMS *Euryalus*, Captain Thomas Dundas (1765 - 1841) of HMS *Naiad*, Captain William Prowse (1752 - 1826) of HMS *Sirius*, and Captain Thomas Bladen Capel (1776 - 1853) of HMS *Phoebe*.

admonishing them against firing a single shot without being sure of their object; and expressed himself to the Officers highly satisfied with the arrangements made at their respective stations.

It was now plainly perceived by all on board the Victory, that from the very compact line which the Enemy had formed, they were determined to make one great effort to recover in some measure their long-lost naval reputation. They wore in succession about twenty minutes past seven o'clock; and stood on the larboard tack, with their heads toward Cadiz. They kept a good deal of sail set; steering about two points from the wind, with topsails shivering. Their van was particularly closed, having the Santissima Trinidada[48] and the Bucentaur[49] the ninth and tenth ships, the latter the flag-ship of Admiral VILLENEUVE[50]: but as the Admirals of the Combined Fleets declined shewing their flags till the heat of the battle was over, the former of these ships was only distinguished from the rest by her having four decks; and Lord NELSON ordered the Victory to be steered for her bow.

Admiral Villeneuve.
Gemälde von Vertier.
(Nach einer Photographie aus der Sammlung P. Lafond.)

Several Officers of the ship now communicated to each other their sentiments of anxiety for HIS LORDSHIP'S personal safety, to which every other consideration seemed to give way. Indeed all were confident of gaining a glorious victory, but the apprehensions for HIS LORDSHIP were great and general; and the

---

[48] *Nuestra Señora de la Santísima Trinidad* launched in 1767 as a three-decker (like HMS *Victory*), modified in 1795 to a four-decker, making her the largest ship at Trafalgar carrying 136 guns.

[49] *Bucentaure* was launched in 1803, carrying 80 guns at Trafalgar.

[50] Pierre-Charles-Jean-Baptiste-Silvestre de Villeneuve (1763 – 1806). During the French Revolution he dropped the 'de' from his name to show his support (and to help avoid the guillotine that so many of his fellow officers met).

Surgeon made known to Doctor SCOTT his fears that HIS LORDSHIP would be made the object of the Enemy's marksmen, and his desire that he might be entreated by somebody to cover the stars on his coat with a handkerchief. Doctor SCOTT and Mr. SCOTT (Public Secretary)[51] both observed, however, that such a request would have no effect; as they knew HIS LORDSHIP'S sentiments on the subject so well, that they were sure he would be highly displeased with whoever should take the liberty of recommending any change in his dress on this account: and when the Surgeon declared to Mr. SCOTT that he would avail himself of the opportunity of making his sick-report for the day,[52] to submit his sentiments to the Admiral, Mr. SCOTT replied, *"Take care, Doctor, what you are about; I would not be the man to mention such a matter to him."* The Surgeon notwithstanding persisted in his design, and remained on deck to find a proper opportunity for addressing His LORDSHIP; but this never occurred: as His LORDSHIP continued occupied with the Captains of the frigates (to whom he was explaining his intentions respecting the services they were to perform during the battle) till a short time before the Enemy—opened their fire on the Royal Sovereign[53], when Lord NELSON ordered all persons not stationed on the quarter-deck or poop to repair to their proper

---

[51] **John Scott (1764 – 1805, killed at Trafalgar).**

[52] The Victory's sick-report for this day numbered only ten convalescents, who all attended their respective quarters during the battle; and the whole Fleet was in a high state of health. Indeed the excellent health enjoyed by the crew of the Victory from December 1804 up to this period, is perhaps unprecedented: and is attributable solely to Captain HARDY'S attention to their subordination, temperance, warm clothing, and cleanliness; together with the means daily adopted to obviate the effects of moisture, and to accomplish the thorough ventilation of every part of the ship.

The Victory arrived at Spithead from the memorable and arduous chace of the Enemies' Fleets to Egypt and the West Indies, in August 1805: and notwithstanding the operation of the unfavourable circumstances of rapid change of climate, and the privation of refreshments experienced in that chace, as well as frequent increase of numbers (as in the West Indies there were at one time embarked in her above 990 souls), there was not now a single hospital-patient on board, nor did any occur during the several weeks of her stay in England; with which Lord NELSON expressed himself highly pleased when he joined the ship again, on the 14th of September, at St. Helen's. The Victory's casualties from the 29th of December 1804 to the 20th of October following, were only five fatal cases (one of these by accidental injury), and two patients sent to a naval hospital.

[53] **Launched in 1786, she was a three-decker carrying 100 guns at Trafalgar, under the flag of Cuthbert Collingwood and captained by Edward Rotherham 1753 – 1830).**

quarters; and the Surgeon, much concerned at this disappointment, retired from the deck with several other Officers.[54]

The boats on the quarters of the ship, being found in the way of the guns, were now lowered, down, and towed astern. Captain BLACKWOOD, of the Euryalus, remained on board the Victory till a few minutes before the Enemy began to fire upon her. He represented to His LORDSHIP, that his flag-ship would be singled out and much pressed by the Enemy; and suggested the propriety therefore of permitting one or two ships of his line to go ahead of the Victory, and lead her into action, which might be the means of drawing in some measure the Enemy's attention from her. To this Lord NELSON assented, and at half past nine o'clock he ordered the Temeraire[55] and Leviathan[56] by signal (the former of which ships, being close to the Victory, was hailed by His LORDSHIP) to go ahead for that purpose; but from the light breeze that prevailed they were unable, notwithstanding their utmost efforts, to attain their intended stations. Captain BLACKWOOD foresaw that this would be the case; and as the Victory still continued to carry all her sail, he wished Captain HARDY to acquaint His LORDSHIP, that unless her sail was in some degree shortened, the two ships just mentioned could not succeed in getting ahead previously to the Enemy's line being forced: this however Captain HARDY declined doing, as he conceived His LORDSHIP'S ardour to get into battle would on no account suffer such a measure.[57]

About half an hour before the Enemy opened their fire, the memorable telegraphic signal was made, that "*ENGLAND EXPECTS EVERY MAN WILL DO HIS DUTY*," which was spread and received throughout the Fleet with enthusiasm. It is impossible adequately to describe by any language, the lively emotions excited in the crew of the Victory when this propitious communication was made known to them: confidence and resolution were strongly pourtrayed in the countenance of all; and

---

[54] It has been reported, but erroneously, that His LORDSHIP was actually requested by his Officers to change his dress, or to cover his stars.

[55] **HMS *Temeraire* was launched in 1790, and at Trafalgar carried 98 guns and was under the command of Captain Eliab Harvey (1758 – 1830).**

[56] **HMS *Leviathan* was launched in 1790, and at Trafalgar carried 74 guns and was under the command of Captain Henry William Bayntun (1766 - 1840).**

[57] His LORDSHIP just at this time found fault with the Officer commanding on the forecastle, because the lee (or starboard) lower studding-sail had not been set sooner; a circumstance which, though trivial in itself, shews how well Captain HARDY knew His LORDSHIP'S sentiments.

the sentiment generally expressed to each other was, that they would prove to their Country that day, how well British seamen could "*do their duty*" when led to battle by their revered Admiral. The signal was afterwards made to "*prepare to anchor after the close of the day;*" and union-jacks[58] were hoisted at the fore-topmast and top-gallant-stays of each ship, to serve as a distinction from the Enemy's, in conformity with orders previously issued by the Commander in Chief. By HIS LORDSHIP'S directions also, the different divisions of the Fleet hoisted the St. George's or white ensign, being the colours of the Commander in Chief: this was done to prevent confusion from occurring during the battle, through a variety of national flags.

The Royal Sovereign now made the signal by telegraph, that "*the Enemy's Commander in Chief was in a frigate.*" This mistake arose from one of their frigates making many signals. Lord NELSON ordered his line to be steered about two points more to the northward than that of his Second in Command, for the purpose of cutting off the retreat of the Enemy's van to the port of Cadiz; which was the reason of the three leading ships of Admiral COLLINGWOOD's line being engaged with the Enemy previously to those of the Commander in Chief's line.

The Enemy began to fire on the Royal Sovereign at thirty minutes past eleven o'clock; in ten minutes after which she got under the stern of the St. Anna[59], and commenced a fire on her. Lieutenant PASCO[60], Signal Officer of the Victory, was heard to say while looking through his glass, "*There is a top-gallant-yard gone.*" His LORDSHIP eagerly asked, "*Whose top-gallant-yard is that gone? Is it the Royal Sovereign's?*" and on being answered by Lieutenant PASCO in the negative, and that it was the Enemy's, he smiled, and said: "*COLLINGWOOD is doing well.*"[61]

---

[58] **The Union Jack, or Union Flag, was implemented in 1801 and combines the blue of the Cross of St. Andrew (Scotland), the Cross of St. Patrick (Ireland), and the Cross of St. George (England).**

[59] **The *Santa Ana*, launched in 1784 and at Trafalgar carried 112 guns. She carried the flag of Vice-Admiral Ignacio María de Álava y Navarrete and was captained by Don José de Gardoqui.**

[60] **John Pasco (1744 – 1853).**

[61] His LORDSHIP in a few minutes after this called Lieutenant PASCO, Mr. OGILVIE, and some other Officers, near him, and desired them to set their watches by the time of that which His LORDSHIP wore.

At fifty minutes past eleven the Enemy opened their fire on the Commander in Chief. They shewed great coolness in the commencement of the battle; for as the Victory approached their line, their ships lying immediately ahead of her and across her bows fired only one gun at a time, to ascertain whether she was yet within their range. This was frequently repeated by eight or nine of their ships, till at length a shot passed through the Victory's main-top-gallant-sail; the hole in which being discovered by the Enemy, they immediately opened their broadsides, supporting an awful and tremendous fire. In a very short time afterwards, Mr. SCOTT, Public Secretary to the Commander in Chief, was killed by a cannon-shot while in conversation with Captain HARDY. Lord NELSON being then near them, Captain ADAIR of the Marines[62], with the assistance of a Seaman, endeavoured to remove the body from His LORDSHIP'S sight: but he had already observed the fall of his Secretary; and now said with anxiety, "*Is that poor SCOTT that is gone?*" and on being answered in the affirmative by Captain ADAIR, he replied, "*Poor fellow!*"

LORD NELSON and Captain HARDY walked the quarter-deck in conversation for some time after this, while the Enemy kept up an incessant raking fire. A double-headed shot struck one of the parties of Marines drawn up on the poop, and killed eight of them; when His LORDSHIP, perceiving this, ordered Captain ADAIR, to disperse his men round the ship, that they might not suffer so much from being together. In a few minutes afterwards a shot struck the fore-brace-bits on the quarter-deck, and passed between Lord NELSON and Captain HARDY; a splinter from the bits bruising Captain HARDY'S foot, and tearing the buckle from his shoe. They both instantly stopped; and were observed by the Officers on deck to survey each other with inquiring looks, each supposing the other to be wounded. His LORDSHIP then smiled, and said: "*This is too warm work, HARDY, to last long;*" and declared that "*through all the battles he had been in, he had never witnessed more cool courage than was displayed by the Victory's crew on this occasion.*"

The Victory by this time, having approached close to the Enemy's van, had suffered very severely without firing a single gun: she had lost about twenty men killed, and had about thirty wounded. Her mizen-topmast, and all her studding-sails and their booms, on both sides were shot away; the Enemy's fire being chiefly directed at her rigging, with a view to disable her before she could close with them.[63] At four

---

[62] **Captain of Marines Charles William Adair (1776 - 1805, killed at Trafalgar).**

[63] The Enemy's fire continued to be pointed so high throughout the engagement, that the Victory did not lose a man on her lower deck; and had only two wounded on that deck, and these by musket-bulls.

minutes past twelve o'clock she opened her fire, from both sides of her decks, upon the Enemy; when Captain HARDY represented to His LORDSHIP, that "*it appeared impracticable to pass through the Enemy's line without going on board some one of their ships.*" Lord NELSON answered, "*I cannot help it: it does not signify which we run on board of; go on board which you please; take your choice.*"

At twenty minutes past twelve, the tiller-ropes being shot away, Mr. ATKINSON[64], the Master, was ordered below to get the helm put to port; which being done, the Victory was soon run on board the Redoutable[65] of seventy-four guns. On coming alongside and nearly on board of her, that ship fired her broadside into the Victory, and immediately let down her lower-deck ports; which, as has been since learnt, was done to prevent her from being boarded through them by the Victory's crew. She never fired a great gun after this single broadside. A few minutes after this, the Temeraire fell likewise on board of the Redoutable, on the side opposite to the Victory; having also an Enemy's ship, said to be La Fougueux[66], on board of her on her other side: so that the extraordinary and unprecedented circumstance occurred here, of four ships of the line being on board of each other in the heat of battle; forming as compact a tier as if they had been moored together, their heads lying all the same way. The Temeraire, as was just before mentioned, was between the Redoutable and La Fougueux. The Redoutable commenced a heavy fire of musketry from the tops, which was continued for a considerable time with destructive effect to the Victory's crew: her great guns however being silent, it was supposed at different times that she had surrendered; and in consequence of this opinion, the Victory twice ceased firing upon her, by orders transmitted from the quarter-deck.

At this period, scarcely a person in the Victory escaped unhurt who was exposed to the Enemy's musketry; but there were frequent huzzas and cheers heard from between the decks, in token of the surrender of different of the Enemy's ships. An incessant fire was kept up from both sides of the Victory; her larboard guns played upon the Santissima Trinidada and the Bucentaur; and the starboard guns of the middle and lower decks were depressed, and fired with a diminished charge of

---

[64] **Thomas Atkinson (1767 – 1836).**

[65] *Redoutable* **was launched in 1791 as** *Suffren*, **renamed in 1795 to** *Redoutable*, **and at Trafalgar carried 74 guns and was under the command of Captain Jean Jacques Etienne Lucas.**

[66] *Fougueux* **was launched in 1785. At Trafalgar she carried 74 guns and was under the command of Louis Alexis Baudoin.**

powder, and three shot each, into the Redoutable. This mode of firing was adopted by Lieutenants WILLIAMS, KING, YULE, and BROWN[67], to obviate the danger of the Temeraire's suffering from the Victory's shot passing through the Redoutable; which must have been the case if the usual quantity of powder, and the common elevation, had been given to the guns.—A circumstance occurred in this situation, which shewed in a most striking manner the cool intrepidity of the Officers and men stationed on the lower deck of the Victory. When the guns, on this deck were run out, their muzzles came into contact with the Redoutable's side; and consequently at every discharge there was reason to fear that the Enemy would take fire, and both the Victory and the Temeraire be involved in her flames. Here then was seen the astonishing spectacle of the fireman of each gun standing ready with a bucket full of water which as soon as his gun was discharged he dashed into the Enemy through the holes made in her side by the shot.

It was from this ship (the Redoutable) that Lord NELSON received his mortal wound. About fifteen minutes past one o'clock, which was in the heat of the engagement, he was walking the middle of the quarter-deck with Captain HARDY, and in the act of turning near the hatchway with his face towards the stern of the Victory, when the fatal ball was fired from the Enemy's mizen-top; which, from the situation of the two ships (lying on board of each other), was brought just abaft, and

rather below, the Victory's main-yard, and of course not more than fifteen yards distant from that part of the deck where His LORDSHIP stood. The ball struck the epaulette on his left shoulder, and penetrated his chest. He fell with his face on the deck. Captain HARDY, who was on his right (the side furthest from the Enemy) and advanced some steps before His LORDSHIP, on turning round, saw the Serjeant Major (SECKER) of Marines[68] with two Seamen raising him from the deck; where he had fallen on the same spot on which, a little before, his Secretary had breathed his last, with whose blood His LORDSHIP's clothes were much soiled. Captain HARDY expressed a hope that he was not severely wounded; to which the gallant Chief replied: "*They have done for me at last, HARDY.*"—"*I hope not,*" answered Captain HARDY. "*Yes,*" replied His LORDSHIP; "*my backbone is shot through.*"

---

[67] **Edward Williams, Andrew King, John Yule, and George Browne (aged 21).**
[68] **James Secker (aged 24).**

CAPTAIN HARDY ordered the Seamen to carry the Admiral to the cockpit[69]; and now two incidents occurred strikingly characteristic of this great man, and strongly marking that energy and reflection which in his heroic mind rose superior even to the immediate consideration of his present awful condition. While the men were carrying him down the ladder from the middle deck, His LORDSHIP observed that the tiller-ropes were not yet replaced; and desired one of the Midshipmen stationed there to go upon the quarter-deck and remind Captain HARDY of that circumstance, and request that new ones should be immediately rove. Having delivered this order, he took his handkerchief from his pocket and covered his face with it, that he might be conveyed to the cockpit at this crisis unnoticed by the crew.

Several wounded Officers, and about forty men, were likewise earned to the Surgeon for assistance just at this time; and some others had breathed their last during their conveyance below. Among the latter were Lieutenant WILLIAM ANDREW RAM[70], and Mr. WHIPPLE Captain's Clerk[71]. The Surgeon had just examined these two Officers, and found that they were dead,[72] when his attention was arrested by several of the wounded calling to him, "*Mr. BEATTY, Lord NELSON is here: Mr. BEATTY, the Admiral is wounded.*"—The Surgeon now, on looking round, saw the handkerchief fall from His LORDSHIP's face; when the stars on his coat, which also had been covered by it, appeared. Mr. BURKE the Purser[73], and the Surgeon, ran immediately to the assistance of His LORDSHIP, and took him from the arms of the Seamen who had carried him below. In conveying him to one of the Midshipmen's births, they stumbled, but recovered themselves without falling. Lord NELSON then inquired who were supporting him; and when the Surgeon informed him, His LORDSHIP replied, "*Ah, Mr. BEATTY! you can do nothing for me. I have but a short time to live: my back is shot through.*" The Surgeon said, "*he hoped the wound was not so dangerous as His LORDSHIP imagined, and that he

---

[69] The cockpit is on the orlop deck of HMS *Victory*.
[70] William Ram was aged 21 at Trafalgar and died during the battle. He is known as the man who was buried twice, as he was buried at sea after the battle and after his body washed ashore, he was then re-buried in Cadiz.
[71] Thomas Whipple was aged 20 at Trafalgar, where he died from '*wind of shot*', where a shot passed close by to him, and the shock-waves from it either wrecked his internal organs or collapsed his lungs, leaving no mark on the body.
[72] The reader may judge of the Surgeon's feelings at this momentous period, when informed that that excellent young Officer Mr. RAM was one of his dearest friends.
[73] **Walter Burke (1736 – 1815).**

might still survive long to enjoy his glorious victory." The Reverend Doctor SCOTT, who had been absent in another part of the cockpit administering lemonade to the wounded, now came instantly to His LORDSHIP; and in the anguish of grief wrung his hands, and said: "Alas, BEATTY, how prophetic you were!" alluding to the apprehensions expressed by the Surgeon for His LORDSHIP's safety previous to the battle.

EMMA, LADY HAMILTON
(From the Stipple Engraving by John Jones after George Romney, 1785)

His LORDSHIP was laid upon a bed, stripped of his clothes, and covered with a sheet. While this was effecting, he said to Doctor SCOTT, "Doctor, I told you so. Doctor, I am gone;" and after a short pause he added in a low voice, "I have to leave Lady HAMILTON, and my adopted daughter HORATIA[74], as a legacy to my Country." The Surgeon then examined the wound, assuring His LORDSHIP that he would not put him to much pain in endeavouring to discover the course of the ball; which he soon found had penetrated deep into the chest, and had probably lodged in the spine. This being explained to His LORDSHIP, he replied, "he was confident his back was shot through." The back was then examined externally, but without any injury being perceived; on which His LORDSHIP was requested by the Surgeon to make him acquainted with all his sensations. He replied, that "he felt a gush of blood every minute within his breast: that he had no feeling in the lower part of his body: and that his breathing was difficult, and attended with very severe pain about that part of the spine where he was confident that the ball had struck; for," said he, "I felt it break my back." These

---

[74] Horatia Nelson was the illegitimate child of Horatio Nelson and Emma Hamilton. She was born in 1801 and lived until 1881, having ten children from her marriage to the Reverend Philip Ward (1795 – 1859). Emma and Nelson were initially listed as her godparents, as she was listed as an orphan of Naples, and then they 'adopted' her after William Hamilton's Death.

symptoms, but more particularly the gush of blood which His LORDSHIP complained of, together with the state of his pulse, indicated to the Surgeon the hopeless situation of the case; but till after the victory was ascertained and announced to His LORDSHIP, the true nature of his wound was concealed by the Surgeon from all on board except only Captain HARDY, Doctor SCOTT, Mr. BURKE, and Messrs. SMITH and WESTEMBURG the Assistant Surgeons[75].

The Victory's crew cheered whenever they observed an Enemy's ship surrender. On one of these occasions, Lord NELSON anxiously inquired what was the cause of it; when Lieutenant PASCO, who lay wounded at some distance from His LORDSHIP, raised himself up, and told him that another ship had struck, which appeared to give him much satisfaction. He now felt an ardent thirst; and frequently called for drink, and to be fanned with paper, making use of these words: "*Fan, fan,*" and "*Drink, drink.*" This he continued to repeat, when he wished for drink or the refreshment of cool air, till a very few minutes before he expired. Lemonade, and wine and water, were given to him occasionally. He evinced great solicitude for the event of the battle, and fears for the safety of his friend Captain HARDY. Doctor SCOTT and Mr. BURKE used every argument they could suggest, to relieve his anxiety. Mr. BURKE told him "*the Enemy were decisively defeated, and that he hoped His LORDSHIP would still live to be himself the bearer of the joyful tidings to his country.*" He replied, "*It is nonsense, Mr. BURKE, to suppose I can live: my sufferings are great, but they will all be soon over.*" Doctor SCOTT entreated His LORDSHIP "*not to despair of living,*" and said "*he trusted that Divine Providence would restore him once more to his dear Country and friends.* "Ah, Doctor!" replied His LORDSHIP, "*it is all over; it is all over.*"

---

[75] **Neil Smith and William Westenburgh.**

Many messages were sent to Captain HARDY by the Surgeon, requesting his attendance on His LORDSHIP; who became impatient to see him, and often exclaimed: "*Will no one bring HARDY to me? He must be killed: he is surely destroyed,*" The Captain's Aide-de-camp, Mr. BULKLEY[76], now came below, and stated that "*circumstances respecting the Fleet required Captain HARDY'S presence on deck, but that he would avail himself of the first favourable moment to visit His LORDSHIP.*" On hearing him deliver this message to the Surgeon, His LORDSHIP inquired who had brought it. Mr. BURKE answered, "*It is Mr. BULKLEY, my Lord.*"— "*It is his voice,*" replied His LORDSHIP: he then said to the young gentleman, "*Remember me to your father.*"

An hour and ten minutes however elapsed, from the time of His LORDSHIP's being wounded, before Captain HARDY's first subsequent interview with him; the particulars of which are nearly as follow. They shook hands affectionately, and Lord NELSON said: "*Well, HARDY, how goes the battle? How goes the day with us?*"— "*Very well, my Lord,*" replied Captain HARDY: "*we have got twelve or fourteen of the Enemy's ships in our possession; but five of their van have tacked, and shew an intention of bearing down upon the Victory. I have therefore called two or three of our fresh ships round us, and have no doubt of giving them a drubbing.*" "*I hope,*" said HIS LORDSHIP, "*none of our ships have struck, HARDY.*"—"*No, my Lord,*" replied Captain HARDY; "*there is no fear of that.*" Lord NELSON then said: "*I am a dead man, HARDY. I am going fast: it will be all over with me soon. Come nearer to me. Pray let my dear Lady HAMILTON have my hair, and all other things belonging to me.*" Mr. BURKE was about to withdraw at the commencement of this conversation; but HIS LORDSHIP, perceiving his intention, desired he would remain. Captain HARDY observed, that "*he hoped Mr. BEATTY could yet hold out some prospect of life.*"—"*Oh! no,*" answered HIS LORDSHIP; "*it is impossible. My back is shot through. BEATTY will tell you so.*" Captain HARDY then returned on deck, and at parting shook hands again with his revered friend and commander.

HIS LORDSHIP now requested the Surgeon, who had been previously absent a short time attending Mr. RIVERS[77], to return to the wounded, and give his assistance to such of them as he could be useful to; "*for,*" said he, "*you can do nothing for me.*" The Surgeon assured him that the Assistant Surgeons were doing every thing that could be effected for those unfortunate men; but on HIS LORDSHIP's several times

---

[76] **Richard Bulkeley (an American aged 18).**
[77] **Midshipman William Rivers (aged 17), the son of the Master Gunner William Rivers (aged 50).**

repeating his injunctions to that purpose, he left him surrounded by Doctor SCOTT, Mr. BURKE, and two of HIS LORDSHIP'S domestics. After the Surgeon had been absent a few minutes attending Lieutenants PEAKE and REEVES of the Marines[78], who were wounded, he was called by Doctor SCOTT to HIS LORDSHIP, who said: "*Ah, Mr. BEATTY! I have sent for you to say, what I forgot to tell you before, that all power of motion and feeling below my breast are gone; and you*" continued he, "*very well know I can live but a short time.*" The emphatic manner in which he pronounced these last words, left no doubt in the Surgeon's mind, that he adverted to the case of a man who had some months before received a mortal injury of the spine on board the Victory, and had laboured under similar privations of sense and muscular motion. The case had made a great impression on Lord NELSON: he was anxious to know the cause of such symptoms, which was accordingly explained to him; and he now appeared to apply the situation and fate of this man to himself.[79] The Surgeon answered, "*My Lord, you told me so before:*" but he now examined the extremities, to ascertain the fact; when HIS LORDSHIP said, "*Ah, BEATTY! I am too certain of it: SCOTT and BURKE have tried it already. You know I am gone.*" The Surgeon replied: "*My Lord, unhappily for our Country, nothing can be done for you;*" and having made this declaration he was so much affected, that he turned round and withdrew a few steps to conceal his emotions. HIS LORDSHIP said: "*I know it. I feel something rising in my breast,*" putting his hand on his left side, "*which tells me I am gone.*" Drink was recommended liberally, and Doctor SCOTT and Mr. BURKE fanned him with paper. He often exclaimed, "*GOD be praised, I have done my duty;*" and upon the Surgeon's inquiring whether his pain was still very great, he declared, "*it continued so very severe, that he wished he was dead. Yet,*" said he in a lower voice, "*one would like to live a little longer, too:*" and after a pause of a few minutes, he added in the same tone, "*What would become of poor Lady HAMILTON, if she knew my situation!*"

THE Surgeon, finding it impossible to render HIS LORDSHIP any further assistance, left him, to attend Lieutenant BLIGH, Messrs. SMITH and WESTPHALL Midshipmen,[80] and some Seamen, recently wounded. Captain HARDY now came to the cockpit to see HIS LORDSHIP a second time, which was after an interval of

---

[78] **James Peake (aged 26), and Lewis Reeves (aged 19).**

[79] The instance here alluded to occurred in the month of July, in the Victory's return to Europe from the West Indies; and the man survived the injury thirteen days. HIS LORDSHIP, during the whole of that time, manifested much anxiety at the protracted sufferings of an individual whose dissolution was certain, and was expected every hour.

[80] **George Bligh (aged 21), Robert Smith (aged 20), and George Westphal (aged 20).**

about fifty minutes from the conclusion of his first visit. Before he quitted the deck, he sent Lieutenant HILLS[81] to acquaint Admiral COLLINGWOOD with the lamentable circumstance of Lord NELSON'S being wounded.[82]—Lord NELSON and Captain HARDY shook hands again: and while the Captain retained HIS LORDSHIP'S hand, he congratulated him even in the arms of Death on his brilliant victory; "*which,*" he said, "*was complete; though he did not know how many of the Enemy were captured, as it was impossible to perceive every ship distinctly. He was certain however of fourteen or fifteen having surrendered.*" HIS LORDSHIP answered, "*That is well, but I bargained for twenty:*" and then emphatically exclaimed, "*Anchor, HARDY, anchor!*" To this the Captain replied: "*I suppose, my Lord, Admiral COLLINGWOOD will now take upon himself the direction of affairs.*"—"*Not while I live, I hope, HARDY!*" cried the dying Chief; and at that moment endeavoured ineffectually to raise himself from the bed. "*No,*" added he; "*do you anchor, HARDY.*" Captain HARDY then said: "*Shall we make the signal, Sir?*"—"*Yes,*" answered HIS LORDSHIP; "*for if I live, I'll anchor.*"[83] The energetic manner in which he uttered these his last orders to Captain HARDY, accompanied with his efforts to raise himself, evinced his determination never to resign the command while he retained the exercise of his transcendant faculties, and that he expected Captain HARDY still to carry into effect the suggestions of his exalted mind; a sense of his duty overcoming the pains of death. He then told Captain HARDY, "*he felt that in a few minutes he should be no more;*" adding in a low tone, "*Don't throw me overboard, HARDY.*" The Captain answered: "*Oh! no, certainly not.*"—"*Then,*" replied HIS LORDSHIP, "*you know what to do:*[84] *and,*" continued he, "*take care of my dear Lady HAMILTON, HARDY; take care of poor Lady HAMILTON. Kiss me, HARDY.*"[85] The Captain now knelt down, and kissed his cheek; when HIS LORDSHIP said, "*Now I am satisfied. Thank GOD, I have done my duty.*" Captain HARDY stood

---

[81] **Alan Hills (aged 25).**

[82] CAPTAIN HARDY deemed it his duty to give this information to Admiral COLLINGWOOD as soon as the fate of the day was decided; but thinking that HIS LORDSHIP might feel some repugnance to this communication, he left directions for Lieutenant HILLS to be detained on deck at his return, till he himself (Captain HARDY) should come up from the cockpit. Lieutenant HILLS was dispatched on this mission from the Victory, at the very time when the Enemy's van ships that had tacked were passing her to windward and firing at her.

[83] Meaning that in case of HIS LORDSHIP'S surviving till all resistance on the part of the Enemy had ceased, Captain HARDY was then to anchor the British Fleet and the prizes, if it should be found practicable.

[84] Alluding to some wishes previously expressed by HIS LORDSHIP to Captain HARDY respecting the place of his interment.

[85] **Yes, "Kiss me." The origin of where he said 'kismet' is unclear, but there were articles published in the 1920's speculating this, despite all the eyewitnesses saying he said, "Kiss me."**

for a minute or two in silent contemplation: he then knelt down again, and kissed HIS LORDSHIP'S forehead. HIS LORDSHIP said: "*Who is that?*" The Captain answered: "*It is HARDY;*" to which HIS LORDSHIP replied, "*GOD bless you, HARDY!*" After this affecting scene Captain HARDY withdrew, and returned to the quarter-deck, having spent about eight minutes in this his last interview with his dying friend.

Lord NELSON now desired Mr. CHEVALIER[86], his Steward, to turn him upon his right side; which being effected, HIS LORDSHIP said: "*I wish I had not left the deck, for I shall soon be gone.*" He afterwards became very low; his breathing was oppressed, and his voice faint. He said to Doctor SCOTT, "*Doctor, I have not been a great sinner;*" and after a short pause, "*Remember, that I leave Lady HAMILTON and my Daughter HORATIA as a legacy to my Country: and,*" added he, "*never forget HORATIA.*" His thirst now increased; and he called for "*Drink, drink,*" "*Fan, fan,*" and "*Rub, rub:*" addressing himself in the last case to Doctor SCOTT, who had been rubbing HIS LORDSHIP'S breast with his hand, from which he found some relief. These words he spoke in a very rapid manner, which rendered his articulation difficult: but he every now and then, with evident increase of pain, made a greater effort with his vocal powers, and pronounced distinctly these last words: "*Thank GOD, I have done my duty;*" and this great sentiment he continued to repeat as long as he was able to give it utterance.

HIS LORDSHIP became speechless in about fifteen minutes after Captain HARDY left him. Doctor SCOTT and Mr. BURKE, who had all along sustained the bed under his shoulders (which raised him in nearly a semi-recumbent posture, the only one that was supportable to him), forbore to disturb him by speaking to him; and when he had remained speechless about five minutes, HIS LORDSHIP'S Steward went to the Surgeon, who had been a short time occupied with the wounded in another part of the cockpit, and stated his apprehensions that HIS LORDSHIP was dying. The Surgeon immediately repaired to him, and found him on the verge of dissolution. He knelt down by his side, and took up his hand; which was cold, and the pulse gone from the wrist. On the Surgeon's feeling his forehead, which was likewise cold, HIS LORDSHIP opened his eyes, looked up, and shut them again. The Surgeon again left him, and returned to the wounded who required his assistance; but was not absent five minutes before the Steward announced to him that "*he believed HIS LORDSHIP had expired.*" The Surgeon returned, and found that the report was

---

[86] **Henry Lew Chevalier.**

but too well founded: HIS LORDSHIP had breathed his last, at thirty minutes past four o'clock; at which period Doctor SCOTT was in the act of rubbing HIS LORDSHIP'S breast, and Mr. BURKE supporting the bed under his shoulders.[87]

Thus died this matchless Hero, after performing, in a short but brilliant and well-filled life, a series of naval exploits unexampled in any age of the world. None of the sons of Fame ever possessed greater zeal to promote the honour and interest of his King and Country; none ever served them with more devotedness and glory, or with more successful and important results. His character will for ever cast a lustre over the annals of this nation, to whose enemies his very name was a terror. In the battle off CAPE ST. VINCENT, though then in the subordinate station of a Captain, his unprecedented personal prowess will long be recorded with admiration among his profession. The shores of ABOUKIR and COPENHAGEN subsequently witnessed those stupendous achievements which struck the whole civilized world with astonishment. Still these were only preludes to the BATTLE OF TRAFALGAR: in which he shone with a majesty of dignity as far surpassing even his own former renown, as that renown had already exceeded every thing else to be found in the pages of naval history; the transcendantly brightest star in a galaxy of heroes. His splendid example will operate as an everlasting impulse to the enterprising genius of the British Navy.[88]

From the time of HIS LORDSHIP'S being wounded till his death, a period of about two hours and forty-five minutes elapsed; but a knowledge of the decisive victory which was gained, he acquired of Captain HARDY within the first hour-and-a-quarter of this period. A partial cannonade, however, was still maintained, in consequence of the Enemy's running ships passing the British at different points; and the last distant guns which were fired at their van ships that were making off, were heard a minute or two before His LORDSHIP expired.

---

[87] It must occur to the reader, that from the nature of the scene passing in the cockpit, and the noise of the guns, the whole of His LORDSHIP'S expressions could not be borne in mind, nor even distinctly heard, by the different persons attending him. The most interesting parts are here detailed.

[88] Immediately after HIS LORDSHIP expired, Captain HARDY went on board the Royal Sovereign, to communicate the melancholy event, and the nature of HIS LORDSHIP'S last orders, to Admiral COLLINGWOOD.

A steady and continued fire was kept up by the Victory's starboard guns on the Redoutable, for about fifteen minutes after Lord NELSON was wounded; in which short period Captain ADAIR and about eighteen Seamen and Marines were killed, and Lieutenant BLIGH, Mr. PALMER Midshipman[89], and twenty Seamen and Marines, wounded, by the Enemy's musketry alone. The Redoutable had been on fire twice, in her fore-chains and on her forecastle: she had likewise succeeded in throwing a few hand-grenades into the Victory, which set fire to some ropes and canvas on the booms. The cry of "*Fire!*" was now circulated throughout the ship, and even reached the cockpit, without producing the degree of sensation which might be expected on such an awful occasion: the crew soon extinguished the fire on the booms, and then immediately turned their attention to that on board the Enemy; which they likewise put out by throwing buckets of water from the gangway into the Enemy's chains and forecastle, thus furnishing another admirable instance of deliberate intrepidity. At thirty minutes past one o'clock, the Redoutable's musketry having ceased, and her colours being struck, the Victory's men endeavoured to get on board her: but this was found impracticable; for though the two ships were still in contact, yet the top-sides or upper-works of both fell in so much on their upper decks, that there was a great space (perhaps fourteen feet or more) between their gangways; and the Enemy's ports being down, she could not be boarded from the Victory's lower nor middle deck. Several Seamen volunteered their services to Lieutenant QUILLIAM[90], to jump overboard, swim under the Redoutable's bows, and endeavour to get up there; but Captain HARDY refused to permit this. The prize however, and the Victory, fell off from each other; and their separation was believed to be the effect of the concussion produced by the Victory's fire, assisted by the helm of the latter being put to starboard.

MESSRS. OGILVIE, and COLLINGWOOD[91], Midshipmen of the Victory, were sent in a small boat to take charge of the prize, which they effected.[92] After this, the ships of the Enemy's van that had shewn a disposition to attack the Victory, passed to windward; and fired their broadsides not only into her and the Temeraire, but also

---

[89] **Alexander Palmer (aged 21).**

[90] **Eventually Captain John Quilliam (1771 – 1829) from the Isle of Man.**

[91] **Edward Collingwood (aged 21).**

[92] The Redoutable lay alongside and still foul of the Temeraire for some time after this, and till several Seamen were sent from the latter to the assistance of the two Officers and men belonging to the Victory who had before taken possession of the prize.

into the French and Spanish captured ships indiscriminately: and they were seen to back or shiver their topsails for the purpose of doing this with more precision.[93]

The two Midshipmen of the Victory had just boarded the Redoutable, and got their men out of the boat, when a shot from the Enemy's van ships that were making off cut the boat adrift. About ten minutes after taking possession of her, a Midshipman came to her from the Temeraire; and had hardly ascended the poop, when a shot from one of those ships took off his leg.

The Fighting Temeraire, tugged to her last berth to be broken up, 1838. JMW Turner, 1838, Rijksmuseum RP-F-2001-7-58-44

The French Officers, seeing the firing continued on the prize by their own countrymen, entreated the English Midshipmen to quit the deck, and accompany them below. The unfortunate Midshipman of the Temeraire was carried to the French Surgeon, who was ordered to give his immediate attendance to him in preference to his own wounded: his leg was amputated, but he died the same night. The Redoutable suffered so much from shot received between wind and

---

[93] These were the ships commanded by Admiral DUMANNOIR, and afterwards captured by the squadron under the command of Sir RICHARD STRACHAN. They were nearly half an hour in passing to windward, during the whole of which time they continued firing on the British ships.

water, that she sunk while in tow of the Swiftsure[94] on the following evening, when the gale came on; and out of a crew originally consisting of more than eight hundred men, only about a hundred and thirty were saved: but she had lost above three hundred in the battle.[95]

It is by no means certain, though highly probable, that Lord NELSON was particularly aimed at by the Enemy. There were only two Frenchmen left alive in the mizen-top of the Redoutable at the time of His LORDSHIP'S being wounded, and by the hands of one of these he fell. These men continued firing at Captains HARDY and ADAIR, Lieutenant ROTELY[96] of the Marines, and some of the Midshipman on the Victory's poop, for some time afterwards. At length one of them was killed by a musket-ball: and on the other's then attempting to make his escape from the top down the rigging, Mr. POLLARD (Midshipman)[97] fired his musket at him, and shot him in the back; when he fell dead from the shrouds, on the Redoutable's poop.

The Writer of this will not attempt to depict the heart-rending sorrow, and melancholy gloom, which pervaded the breast and the countenance of every individual on board the Victory when His LORDSHIP'S death became generally known. The anguish felt by all for such a loss, rendered doubly heavy to them, is more easy to be conceived than described: by his lamented fall they were at once deprived of their adored commander, and their friend and patron.

The battle was fought in soundings about sixteen miles to the westward of Cape Trafalgar; and if fortunately there had been more wind in the beginning of the action, it is very probable that Lord NELSON would still have been saved to his Country, and that every ship of the line composing the Combined Fleets would have been either captured or destroyed: for had the Victory been going fast through the water, she must have dismasted the Redoutable, and would of course

---

[94] **HMS *Swiftsure* was launched in 1804 and at Trafalgar carried 74 guns under the command of Captain William Rutherford.**

[95] About twenty of the Redoutable's guns were dismounted in the action. Those on that side of her lower deck opposed to the Victory, were all dismounted except five or six.

[96] **Lewis Roteley (aged 20).**

[97] **John Pollard (aged 18).**

have passed on to attack another ship; consequently His LORDSHIP would not have been so long nor so much exposed to the Enemy's musketry. From the same circumstance of there being but little wind, several of the Enemy's ships made off before the rear and bad-sailing ships of the British lines could come up to secure them.

THE Victory had no musketry in her tops: as His LORDSHIP had a strong aversion to small arms being placed there, from the danger of their setting fire to the sails; which was exemplified by the destruction of the French ship L'Achille[98] in this battle. It is a species of warfare by which individuals may suffer, and now and then a Commander be picked off: but it never can decide the fate of a general engagement; and a circumstance in many respects similar to that of the Victory's running on board of the Redoutable, may not occur again in the course of centuries. The loss sustained by the Victory amounted to fifty-five killed, and a hundred and two wounded;[99] and it is highly honourable to the discipline and established regulations of the ship, that not one casualty from accident occurred on board during the engagement.

On the day after the battle, as soon as circumstances permitted the Surgeon to devote a portion of his attention to the care of Lord NELSON'S honoured Remains, measures were adopted to preserve them as effectually as the means then on board the Victory allowed. On the Surgeon's examining the nature of the wound, and the course of the ball, a quantity of blood was evacuated from the left side of the breast: none had escaped before. The ball was traced by a probe to the spine, but its lodgment could not at that time be discovered. There was no lead on board to make a coffin: a cask called a leaguer, which is of the largest size on shipboard, was therefore chosen for the reception of the Body; which, after the hair had been cut off, was stripped of the clothes except the shirt, and put into it, and the Cask was then filled with brandy.[100]

---

[98] **The French *Achille* was launched in 1804 and at Trafalgar carried 74 guns and was under the command of Louis-Gabriel Deniéport.**

[99] Many of those who were slightly wounded did not apply for assistance till after the public return of killed and wounded had been transmitted to Admiral COLLINGWOOD, which therefore reports a smaller number than here stated.

[100] Brandy was recommended by the Surgeon in preference to rum, of which spirit also there was plenty on board. This circumstance is here noticed, because a very general but erroneous opinion was found to prevail on the Victory's arrival in

In the evening after this melancholy task was accomplished, the gale came on with violence from the south-west, and continued that night and the succeeding day without any abatement. During this boisterous weather, Lord NELSON'S Body remained under the charge of a sentinel on the middle deck. The cask was placed on its end, having a closed aperture at its top and another below; the object of which was, that as a frequent renewal of the spirit was thought necessary, the old could thus be drawn off below and a fresh quantity introduced above, without moving the cask, or occasioning the least agitation of the Body. On the 24th there was a disengagement of air from the Body to such a degree, that the sentinel became alarmed on seeing the head of the cask raised: he therefore applied to the Officers, who were under the necessity of having the cask spiled to give the air a discharge. After this, no considerable collection of air took place. The spirit was drawn off once, and the cask filled again, before the arrival of the Victory at Gibraltar (on the 28th of October): where spirit of wine was procured; and the cask, shewing a deficit produced by the Body's absorbing a considerable quantity of the brandy[101], was then filled up with it.

On the 29th the Victory's Seamen and Marines dangerously wounded in the action, were sent on shore to the naval hospital at Gibraltar. The interval between this day and the 2nd of November was employed in repairing the damage sustained by the ship, erecting jury-masts, fitting her rigging, and completing her in every respect for the voyage to England. On the 2nd of November, preparations were made on board to receive the wounded from the hospital, who had unanimously entreated Captain HARDY not to leave them behind: but their embarkation could not be effected this day; and the Victory being ordered to quit the anchorage in Gibraltar

---

England, that rum preserves the dead body from decay much longer and more perfectly than any other spirit, and ought therefore to have been used: but the fact is quite the reverse, for there are several kinds of spirit much better for that purpose than rum; and as their appropriateness in this respect arises from their degree of strength, on which alone their antiseptic quality depends, brandy is superior. Spirit of wine, however, is certainly by far the best, when it can be procured.

[101] **On May 25th, 1798, Captain Thomas Byard (1743 – 1798) took command of HMS *Foudroyant*. He died at sea just five months later on October the 31st. The decision was made to preserve his body using brandy whilst the ship made for Plymouth so he could be buried on land. In June the following year, Nelson took the *Foudroyant* as his flag ship, with Hardy as his captain. It is not unreasonable to assume that talk over the dinner table would at some stage have turned to the pickling of Byard.**

Bay, to make room for the disabled ships and prizes daily arriving, she sailed in the evening for Tetuan Bay, for the purpose of taking on board a supply of fresh water, and awaiting there a favourable wind to pass the Straits. During the night however, and before the Victory gained the coast of Barbary, the wind, which had blown for several days from the west, shifted to the eastward, and a fresh breeze sprung up; she therefore changed her course, and stood back again for Gibraltar, where she arrived early in the morning. She then lay-to in the bay without anchoring, and the boats were immediately sent on shore for the wounded; who were all brought off by noon, except five of the worst cases who could not be removed.[102] In the afternoon the Victory and Belleisle sailed from Gibraltar Bay, and passed through the Straits during the night of the 4th. The next day at noon they joined the squadron under the command of Admiral COLLINGWOOD, then cruising off Cadiz; from which they parted company the same evening, and pursued their course together for England.

When the Victory had proceeded some weeks on her voyage, adverse winds and tempestuous weather having prolonged the passage much beyond the period that is generally expected, it was thought proper to draw off the spirit from the cask containing Lord NELSON'S Body, and renew it; and this was done twice. On these occasions brandy was used in the proportion of two-thirds to one of spirit of wine.

At length the Victory arrived at Spithead[103], after a tedious passage of nearly five weeks from Gibraltar: and as no instructions respecting His LORDSHIP'S Remains were received at Portsmouth while the ship remained there, and orders being transmitted to Captain HARDY for her to proceed to the Nore, the Surgeon represented to him the necessity of examining the state of the Body; common report giving reason to believe that it was intended to lie in state at Greenwich Hospital, and to be literally exposed to the public. On the 11th of December therefore, the day on which the Victory sailed from Spithead for the Nore, Lord NELSON'S Body was taken from the cask in which it had been kept since the day

---

[102] Of the Victory's wounded, three died before she reached Gibraltar, one on the day of her arrival there, and another at the naval hospital at that place a few days afterwards: all the rest got well on board except the five left at Gibraltar, and five others not perfectly recovered from their wounds in January following; when the Victory being put out of commission at Chatham, they were sent to the Sussex hospital-ship at Sheerness.

[103] **Spithead is the deep-water anchorage in the Solent between Portsmouth and the Isle of Wight.**

after his death. On inspecting it externally, it exhibited a state of perfect preservation, without being in the smallest degree offensive. There were, however, some appearances that induced the Surgeon to examine the condition of the bowels; which were found to be much decayed, and likely in a short time to communicate the process of putrefaction to the rest of the Body: the parts already injured were therefore removed. It was at this time that the fatal ball was discovered: it had passed through the spine, and lodged in the muscles of the back, towards the right side, and a little below the shoulder-blade. A very considerable portion of the gold-lace, pad, and lining of the epaulette, with a piece of the coat, was found attached to the ball: the lace of the epaulette was as firmly so, as if it had been inserted into the metal while in a state of fusion.[104]

The Ball

---

[104] The ball was not fired from a rifle piece.

The following is the professional Report on HIS LORDSHIP'S wound and death, made by the Surgeon on this occasion;

His Majesty's Ship Victory, at Sea,

11th December, 1805.

About the middle of the action with the Combined Fleets on the 21st of October last, the late illustrious Commander in Chief Lord NELSON was mortally wounded in the left breast by a musket-ball, supposed to be fired from the mizen-top of La Redoutable French ship of the line, which the Victory fell on board of early in the battle. HIS LORDSHIP was in the act of turning on the quarter-deck with his face towards the Enemy, when he received his wound: he instantly fell; and was carried to the cockpit, where he lived about two hours.[105] On being brought below, he complained of acute pain about the sixth or seventh dorsal vertebra, and of privation of sense and motion of the body and inferior extremities. His respiration was short and difficult; pulse weak, small, and irregular. He frequently declared his back was shot through, that he felt every instant a gush of blood within his breast, and that he had sensations which indicated to him the approach of death. In the course of an hour his pulse became indistinct, and was gradually lost in the arm. His extremities and forehead became soon afterwards cold. He retained his wonted energy of mind, and exercise of his faculties, till the last moment of his existence; and when the victory as signal as decisive was announced to him, he expressed his pious acknowledgments, and heart-felt satisfaction at the glorious event, in the most emphatic language. He then delivered his last orders with his usual precision, and in a few minutes afterwards expired without a struggle.

Course and site of the Ball, as ascertained since death.

The ball struck the fore part of HIS LORDSHIP'S epaulette; and entered the left shoulder immediately before the processus acromion scapulae, which it slightly fractured. It then descended obliquely into the thorax, fracturing the second and third ribs: and after penetrating the left lobe of the lungs, and dividing in its passage a large branch of the pulmonary artery, it entered the left side of the spine between the sixth and seventh dorsal vertebræ, fractured the left transverse process of the sixth dorsal vertebra, wounded the medulla spinalis, and fracturing the right transverse process of the seventh vertebra, made its way from the right

---

[105] It was not deemed necessary to insert in this Report the precise time which HIS LORDSHIP survived his wound. This, as before stated, was in reality two hours and three quarters.

side of the spine, directing its course through the muscles of the back; and lodged therein, about two inches below the inferior angle of the right scapula. On removing the ball, a portion of the gold-lace and pad of the epaulette, together with a small piece of HIS LORDSHIP'S coat, was found firmly attached to it.[106]

W. BEATTY.

THE ADMIRALTY.

The Admiralty, between Trafalgar Square and the Horse Guards, was once known as Wallingford House, and its present front was built about 1725 by Thomas Ripley, to whom contemptuous reference is made in the "Dunciad;" while fifty years later the stone screen, with its appropriate marine emblems, by Robert Adam, was added. Viewed from the outside, the building, which, it will be noticed, stands back from the road, is not particularly impressive, but its interior is well arranged, though inadequate for present needs; and large new offices have been built in the rear, facing St. James's Park. It was at the Admiralty that Lord Nelson's body lay in state before being interred in St. Paul's Cathedral.

The Remains were wrapped in cotton vestments, and rolled from head to foot with bandages of the same material, in the ancient mode of embalming. The Body was then put into a leaden coffin, filled with brandy holding in solution camphor and

---

[106] FIG. 1. in the annexed Plate represents the Ball in the exact state in which it was extracted. Drawn by Mr. W.E. DEVIS, who was then on board the Victory.
FIG. 2. (drawn also by Mr. DEVIS) shews the Ball in its present state; as set in crystal by Mr. YONGE, and presented to the Writer of this Narrative by Sir THOMAS HARDY.
The Ball, in perforating the epaulette, passed through many of the silk cords supporting the bullions, and through the pad and a doubling of silk besides; as the bag of the pad was composed of yellow silk. This circumstance militates strongly against an opinion entertained by some, that silk possesses in an eminent degree the power of resisting the force, or arresting the velocity, of a musket or pistol ball.

myrrh.[107] This coffin was inclosed in a wooden one, and placed in the after-part of HIS LORDSHIP'S cabin; where it remained till the 21st of December, when an order was received from the Admiralty for the removal of the Body. The coffin that had been made from the mainmast of the French Commander's ship L'Orient[108], and presented to HIS LORDSHIP by his friend Captain HOLLOWELL[109], after the battle of the Nile, being then received on board, the leaden coffin was opened, and the Body taken out; when it was found still in most excellent condition, and completely plastic.

Of the Memorable Victory of the Nile, (after William Anderson 1800), Rijksmuseum RP-P-1948-276A

The features were somewhat tumid, from absorption of the spirit; but on using friction with a napkin, they resumed in a great degree their natural character. All the Officers of the ship, and several of HIS LORDSHIP'S friends, as well as some of Captain HARDY'S, who had come on board the Victory that day from the shore, were present at the time of the Body's being removed from the leaden coffin; and

---

[107] The stock of spirit of wine on board was exhausted and from the sound state of the Body, brandy was judged sufficient for its preservation.
[108] **During the Battle of the Nile, the *L'Orient*, launched in 1791 and carrying 120 guns, exploded.**
[109] **Eventually Admiral Benjamin Hallowell Carew (1761 – 1834).**

witnessed its undecayed state after a lapse of two months since death, which excited the surprise of all who beheld it. This was the last time the mortal part of the lamented Hero was seen by human eyes; as the Body, after being dressed in a shirt, stockings, uniform small-clothes and waistcoat, neckcloth, and night-cap, was then placed in the shell made from L'Orient's mast, and covered with the shrouding. This was inclosed in a leaden coffin; which was soldered up immediately, and put into another wooden shell: in which manner it was sent out of the Victory into Commissioner GREY'S yacht[110], which was hauled alongside for that purpose. In this vessel the revered Remains were conveyed to Greenwich Hospital; attended by the Reverend Doctor SCOTT, and Messrs. TYSON and WHITBY.

LORD NELSON had often talked with Captain HARDY on the subject of his being killed in battle, which appeared indeed to be a favourite topic of conversation with him. He was always prepared to lay down his life in the service of his Country; and whenever it should please Providence to remove him from this world, it was the most ambitious wish of his soul to die in the fight, and in the very hour of a great and signal victory. In this he was gratified: his end was glorious; and he died as he had lived, one of the greatest among men.

The following Prayer, found in HIS LORDSHIP'S memorandum-book,—and written with his own hand on the night of his leaving Merton [111](*right*), at one of the places where he changed horses (supposed to be Guildford) on his way to join the Victory at Portsmouth,—is highly illustrative of those sentiments of combined piety and patriotic heroism with which he was inspired:

---

[110] George Grey (1767 – 1828), and his yacht was called the *Chatham*.

[111] Merton Place was in the borough of Merton, near Wimbledon, London. The house was demolished in 1823 and there is now a housing estate over much of the old estate. If you search for '*Nelson Merton Trail*', you will find a walking route of the area.

Friday Night, 13th September.

Friday night, at half past ten, drove from dear, dear Merton, where I left all which I hold dear in this world, to go to serve my King and Country. May the great GOD whom I adore, enable me to fulfil the expectations of my Country! and if it is His good pleasure that I should return, my thanks will never cease being offered up to the throne of His mercy. But if it is His good providence to cut short my days upon earth, I bow with the greatest submission; relying that He will protect those, so dear to me, that I may leave behind. His will be done!

AMEN, amen, amen.

HIS LORDSHIP had on several occasions told Captain HARDY, that if he should fall in battle in a foreign climate, he wished his body to be conveyed to England; and that if his Country should think proper to inter him at the public expence, he wished to be buried in Saint Paul's, as well as that his monument should be erected there. He explained his reasons for preferring Saint Paul's to Westminster Abbey, which were rather curious: he said that he remembered hearing it stated as an old tradition when he was a boy, that Westminster Abbey was built on a spot where once existed a deep morass; and he thought it likely that the lapse of time would reduce the ground on which it now stands to its primitive state of a swamp, without leaving a trace of the Abbey. He added, that his actual observations confirmed the probability of this event. He also repeated to Captain HARDY several times during the last two years of his life: "*Should I be killed, HARDY, and my Country not bury me, you know what to do with me;*" meaning that his body was in that case to be laid by the side of his Father's, in his native village of Burnham Thorpe in Norfolk: and this, as has been before mentioned he adverted to in his last moments.

An opinion has been very generally entertained, that Lord NELSON'S state of health, and supposed infirmities arising from his former wounds and hard services, precluded the probability of his long surviving the battle of Trafalgar, had he fortunately escaped the Enemy's shot: but the Writer of this can assert that HIS LORDSHIP'S health was uniformly good, with the exception of some slight attacks of indisposition arising from accidental causes; and which never continued above two or three days, nor confined him in any degree with respect to either exercise or regimen:[112] and during the last twelve months of his life, he complained only three times in this way. It is true, that HIS LORDSHIP, about the meridian of life, had been subject to frequent fits of the gout: which disease however, as well as his constitutional tendency to it, he totally overcame by abstaining for the space of nearly two years from animal food, and wine and all other fermented drink; confining his diet to vegetables, and commonly milk and water. And it is also a fact, that early in life, when he first went to sea, he left off the use of salt, which he then believed to be the sole cause of scurvy, and never took it afterwards with his food.

HIS LORDSHIP used a great deal of exercise, generally walking on deck six or seven hours in the day. He always rose early, for the most part shortly after day-break. He breakfasted in summer about six, and at seven in winter: and if not occupied in reading or writing dispatches, or examining into the details of the Fleet, he walked on the quarter-deck the greater part of the forenoon; going down to his cabin occasionally to commit to paper such incidents or reflections as occurred to him during that time, and as might be hereafter useful to the service of his country. He dined generally about half past two o'clock. At his table there were seldom less than eight or nine persons, consisting of the different Officers of the ship: and when the weather and the service permitted, he very often had several of the Admirals and Captains in the Fleet to dine with him; who were mostly invited by signal, the rotation of seniority being commonly observed by HIS LORDSHIP in these invitations. At dinner he was alike affable and attentive to every one: he ate very sparingly himself; the liver and wing of a fowl, and a small plate of macaroni, in general composing his meal, during which he occasionally took a glass of Champagne. He never exceeded four glasses of wine after dinner, and seldom drank three; and even these were diluted with either Bristol or common water.

Few men subject to the vicissitudes of a naval life, equalled HIS LORDSHIP in an habitual systematic mode of living. He possessed such a wonderful activity of mind, as even prevented him from taking ordinary repose, seldom enjoying two hours of uninterrupted sleep; and on several occasions he did not quit the deck during the whole night. At these times he took no pains to protect himself from the effects of wet, or the night-air; wearing only a thin great coat: and he has frequently, after

---

[112] These complaints were the consequence of indigestion, brought on by writing for several hours together. HIS LORDSHIP had one of these attacks from that cause a few days before the battle, but on resuming his accustomed exercise he got rid of it. This attack alarmed him, as he attributed it to sudden and violent spasm; but it was merely an unpleasant symptom (globus hystericus) attending indigestion.

having his clothes wet through with rain, refused to have them changed, saying that the leather waistcoat which he wore over his flannel one would secure him from complaint. He seldom wore boots, and was consequently very liable to have his feet wet. When this occurred he has often been known to go down to his cabin, throw off his shoes, and walk on the carpet in his stockings for the purpose of drying the feet of them. He chose rather to adopt this uncomfortable expedient, than to give his servants the trouble of assisting him to put on fresh stockings; which, from his having only one hand, he could not himself conveniently effect.

From these circumstances it may be inferred, that though Lord NELSON'S constitution was not of that kind which is generally denominated strong, yet it was not very susceptible of complaint from the common occasional causes of disease necessarily attending a naval life. The only bodily pain which HIS LORDSHIP felt in consequence of his many wounds, was a slight rheumatic affection of the stump of his amputated arm on any sudden variation in the state of the weather; which is generally experienced by those who have the misfortune to lose a limb after the middle age. HIS LORDSHIP usually predicted an alteration in the weather with as much certainty from feeling transient pains in this stump[113], as he could by his marine barometer; from the indications of which latter he kept a diary of the atmospheric changes, which was written with his own hand.

HIS LORDSHIP had lost his right eye by a contusion which he received at the siege of Calvi, in the island of Corsica[114]. The vision of the other was likewise considerably impaired: he always therefore wore a green shade over his forehead, to defend this eye from the effect of strong light; but as he was in the habit of looking much through a glass while on deck, there is little doubt, that had he lived a few years longer, and continued at sea, he would have lost his sight totally.

The Surgeon had, on the occasion of opening HIS LORDSHIP'S Body, an opportunity of acquiring an accurate knowledge of the sound and healthy state of the thoracic and abdominal viscera, none of which appeared to have ever been the seat of inflammation or disease. There were no morbid indications to be seen; other than those unavoidably attending the human body six weeks after death, even under circumstances more favourable to its preservation. The heart was small, and dense

---

[113] **He nicknamed his stump his *'fin'*, and he lost his arm at Tenerife in 1797.**
[114] **1794**

in its substance; its valves, pericardium, and the large vessels, were sound, and firm in their structure. The lungs were sound, and free from adhesions. The liver was very small, in its colour natural, firm in its texture, and every way free from the smallest appearance of disorganization. The stomach, as well as the spleen and other abdominal contents, was alike free from the traces of disease. Indeed all the vital parts were so perfectly healthy in their appearance, and so small, that they resembled more those of a youth, than of a man who had attained his forty-seventh year; which state of the body, associated with habits of life favourable to health, gives every reason to believe that HIS LORDSHIP might have lived to a great age.

The immediate cause of HIS LORDSHIP'S death was a wound of the left pulmonary artery, which poured out its blood into the cavity of the chest. The quantity of blood thus effused did not appear to be very great: but as the hemorrhage was from a vessel so near the heart, and the blood was consequently lost in a very short time, it produced death sooner than would have been effected by a larger quantity of blood lost from an artery in a more remote part of the body. The injury done to the spine must of itself have proved mortal, but HIS LORDSHIP might perhaps have survived this alone for two or three days; though his existence protracted even for that short period would have been miserable to himself, and highly distressing to the feelings of all around him.

W. BEATTY.

Battle of Trafalgar, and the Death of Lord Nelson (Edward Orme after William Marshall Craig, 1806), RP-P-OB-19.224

APPENDIX.

INSTRUCTIONS

Issued by LORD NELSON to the Admirals and Captains of his Fleet, several days previous to the Battle.

> *Victory, off Cadiz, 10th of October, 1805.*
>
> GENERAL MEMORANDUM *sent to the Commanders of Ships.*
>
> *Thinking it almost impossible to bring a Fleet of forty sail of the line into a line of battle in variable winds, thick weather, and other circumstances which must occur, without such a loss of time that the opportunity would probably be lost of bringing the Enemy to battle in such a manner as to make the business decisive, I have therefore made up my mind to keep the Fleet in that position of sailing, with the exception of the First and Second in Command, that the order of sailing is to be the order of battle: placing the Fleet in two lines, of sixteen ships each with an advanced squadron of eight of the fastest-sailing two-decked ships; which will always make, if wanted, a line of twenty-four sail, on whichever line the Commander in Chief may direct.*
>
> *The Second in Command will, after my intentions are made known to him, have the entire direction of his line; to make the attack upon the Enemy, and to follow up the blow until they are captured or destroyed.*
>
> *If the Enemy's Fleet should be seen to windward in line of battle, and that the two lines and advanced squadron could fetch them, they will probably be so extended that their van could not succour their rear. I should therefore probably make the Second in Command's signal to lead through about their twelfth ship from their rear; or wherever he could fetch, if not able to get so far advanced. My line would lead through about their centre: and the advanced squadron to cut three or four ships ahead of their centre, so as to ensure getting at their Commander in Chief, on whom every effort must be made to capture.*
>
> *The whole impression of the British Fleet must be, to overpower from two or three ships ahead of their Commander in Chief (supposed to be in the centre) to the rear of their Fleet.*

I will suppose twenty sail of the Enemy's line to be untouched: it must be some time before they could perform a manoeuvre to bring their force compact to attack any part of the British Fleet engaged, or to succour their own ships; which indeed would be impossible, without mixing with the ships engaged. The Enemy's Fleet is supposed to consist of forty-six sail of the line; British, forty:[115] *if either is less, only a proportional number of Enemy's ships are to be cut off; British to be one-fourth superior to the Enemy cut off.*

Something must be left to chance: nothing is sure in a sea-fight, beyond all others; shot will carry away masts and yards of friends as well as foes: but I look with confidence to a victory before the van of the Enemy could succour their rear; and then that the British Fleet would most of them be ready to receive their twenty sail of the line, or to pursue them should they endeavour to make off.

If the van of the Enemy tack, the captured ships must run to leeward of the British Fleet: if the Enemy wear, the British must place themselves between the Enemy and captured, and disabled British ships: and should the Enemy close, I have no fear for the result.

The Second in Command will, in all possible things, direct the movements of his line, by keeping them so compact as the nature of the circumstances will admit. Captains are to look to their particular line as their rallying-point; but in case signals cannot be seen or clearly understood, no Captain can do very wrong if he places his ship alongside that of an Enemy.

Plan of the intended attack from to-windward, the Enemy in line of battle ready to receive an attack:

―――—- *Advanced squadron.}*

――――――— *Weather line.   } British.*

―――――――— *Lee line.   }*

――――――――――――――――――-

Enemy's line.

---

[115] With such an inferiority of force as this, HIS LORDSHIP confidently expected not only to gain a decisive victory, but (to use his own favourite phrase) "*completely to annihilate the Enemy's Fleet!*"

The divisions of the British Fleet will be brought nearly within gun-shot of the Enemy's centre. The signal will be made for the lee line to bear up together; to set all their sail, even studding-sails, in order to get as quickly as possible to the Enemy's line; and to cut through, beginning from the twelfth ship from the Enemy's rear. Some ships may not get through their exact place, but they will always be at hand to assist their friends. If any are thrown in the rear of the Enemy, they will effectually complete the business of twelve sail of the Enemy.

Should the Enemy wear together, or bear up and sail large, still the twelve ships composing in the first position the Enemy's rear, are to be the object of attack of the lee line, unless otherwise directed by the Commander in Chief: which is scarcely to be expected; as the entire management of the lee line, after the intentions of the Commander in Chief are signified, is intended to be left to the Admiral commanding that line.

The remainder of the Enemy's Fleet, thirty-four sail, are to be left to the management of the Commander in Chief; who will endeavour to take care that the movements of the Second in Command are as little interrupted as possible.

NELSON AND BRONTE.

By Command of the Vice Admiral.

JNO. SCOTT.

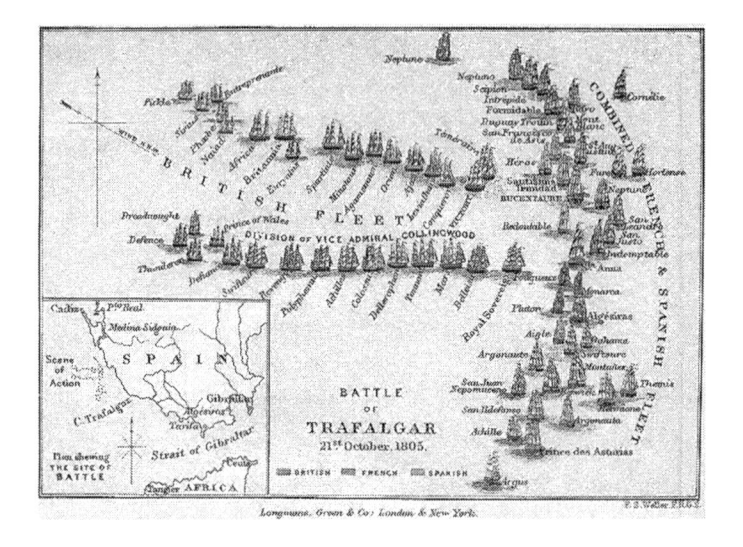

MEMORANDUM BOOK

The following interesting Extracts are faithfully copied from HIS LORDSHIP'S Memorandum Book, written entirely with his own hand.

> *Saturday, September 14th, 1805. At six o'clock arrived at Portsmouth; and having arranged all my business, embarked at the bathing-machines with Mr. ROSE and Mr. CANNING, who dined with me. At two got on board the Victory, at St. Helen's.*

> *Wednesday, Sept. 25th, 1805. Light airs southerly. Saw the rock of Lisbon S.S.E. ten leagues. At sunset the Captain of the Constance came on board, and sent my letters for England to Lisbon, and wrote to Captain SUTTON[116] and the Consul. The Enemy's Fleet had not left Cadiz the 18th of this month, therefore I yet hope they will wait my arrival.*

> *Saturday, Sept. 28th, 1805. Fresh breezes at N.N.W. At day-light bore up, and made sail. At nine saw the Ætna cruising. At noon saw eighteen sail. Nearly calm. In the evening joined the Fleet under Vice Admiral COLLINGWOOD. Saw the Enemy's Fleet in Cadiz, amounting to thirty-five or thirty-six sail of the line.*

> *Sunday, Sept. 29th. Fine weather. Gave out the necessary orders for the Fleet. Sent Euryalus to watch the Enemy with the Hydra off Cadiz.*

> *Wednesday, October 9th. Fresh breezes easterly. Received an account from BLACKWOOD, that the French ships had all bent their top-gallant-sails. Sent the Pickle to him, with orders to keep a good look-out. Sent Admiral COLLINGWOOD the Nelson truth.[117] At night wind westerly.*

---

[116] Of his Majesty's ship Amphion, then in the Tagus.
[117] It is presumed that HIS LORDSHIP here meant the preceding Instructions, which were transmitted the next day to the whole Fleet.

Monday, Oct. 14th. Fine weather: westerly wind. Sent Amphion to Gibraltar and Algiers. Enemy at the harbour's mouth. Placed Defence and Agamemnon from seven to ten leagues west of Cadiz; and Mars and Colossus five leagues east of the Fleet, whose station is from fifteen to twenty west of Cadiz: and by this chain I hope to have a constant communication with the frigates off Cadiz.

Wednesday, Oct. 16th. Moderate breezes westerly. All the forenoon employed forming the Fleet into the order of sailing. At noon fresh breezes W.S.W. and squally. In the evening fresh gales. The Enemy as before, by signal from Weazle.

Thursday, Oct. 17th. Moderate breezes north-westerly. Sent the Donegal to Gibraltar, to get a ground-tier of casks. Received accounts by the Diligent storeship, that Sir RICHARD STRACHAN was supposed in sight of the French Rochefort squadron; which I hope is true.

Friday, Oct. 18th. Fine weather: wind easterly. The Combined Fleets cannot have finer weather to put to sea.

Saturday, Oct. 19th. Fine weather: wind easterly. At half past nine the Mars, being one of the look-out ships, made the signal that the Enemy were coming out of port. Made the signal for a general chace S.E. Wind at south; Cadiz bearing E.S.E. by compass, distance sixteen leagues. At three the Colossus made the signal that the Enemy's Fleet was at sea. In the evening made the signal to observe my motions during the night; for the Britannia, Prince, and Dreadnought, to take stations as most convenient; and for Mars, Orion, Belleisle, Leviathan, Bellerophon, and Polyphemus, to go ahead during the night, and to carry a light, standing for the Straits' mouth.

Sunday, Oct. 20th. Fresh breezes S.S.W., and rainy. Communicated with Phoebe, Defence, and Colossus, who saw near forty sail of ships of war outside of Cadiz yesterday evening; but the wind being southerly, they could not get to the mouth of the Straits. We were between Trafalgar and Cape Spartel. The frigates made the signal that they saw nine sail outside the harbour. Sent the frigates instructions for their guidance; and placed the Defence, Colossus, and Mars, between me and the frigates. At noon fresh gales, and heavy rain: Cadiz N.E. nine leagues. In the afternoon Captain BLACKWOOD telegraphed that the Enemy seemed determined to go to the westward;—and that they shall not do, if in the power of NELSON AND BRONTE to prevent them. At five telegraphed Captain BLACKWOOD, that I relied upon his keeping sight of the Enemy. At five o'clock Naiad made the signal for thirty-one sail of the Enemy N.N.E. The frigates and look-out ship kept sight of the Enemy most admirably all night, and told me by signal which tack they were upon. At eight we wore, and stood to the S.W.; and at four wore and stood to the N.E.

Monday, Oct. 21st. At day-light saw Enemy's Combined Fleets from east to E.S.E. Bore away. Made the signal for order of sailing, and to prepare for battle. The Enemy with their heads to the southward. At seven the Enemy wearing in succession.

Then follow the Prayer and Codicil already inserted in the Narrative, which conclude HIS LORDSHIP'S manuscript.

-- THE END --

The Death of Nelson by Arthur William Devis, 1807

Arthur Devis spent a week onboard HMS *Victory* when she returned to England, and his painting is probably the most recognised of the last moments of Nelson's life. Some artistic licence was taken by Devis, such as including Hardy being present when Nelson drew his last breath.

Courtesy of the Rijksmuseum, RP-P-OB-70.470

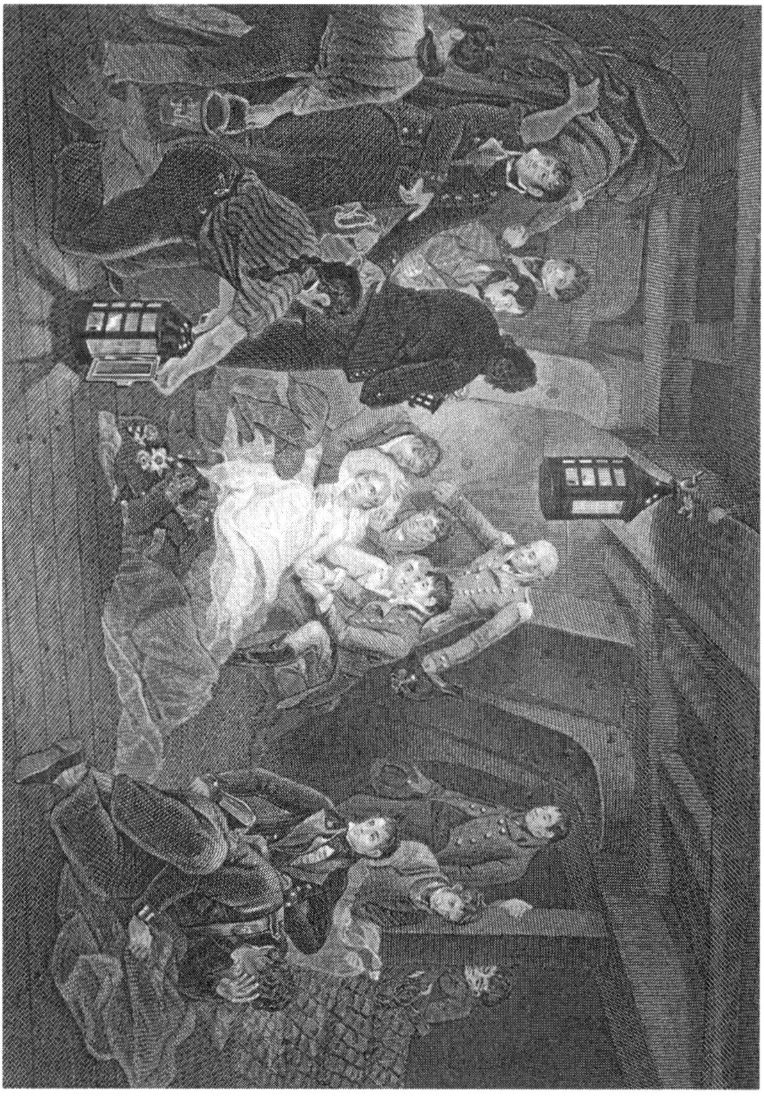

The Battle of Trafalgar – The Aftermath

Though the Battle of Trafalgar was pretty much over by four thirty on that day, an awful lot more happens afterwards that need to be considered when looking at the events.

The first is the storm that hits the battered fleets that evening. Though no British ships had been lost, there was now a race on to make good the damaged prizes so the sailors could get them back to get their rewards as prize money was only paid on the delivery of a ship to a friendly port. Pride in doing your job well is one thing, but under normal circumstances only the admirals and captains would receive the swords and silverware to mark their victories, but get a captured ship back to port and it would be valued with prize monies issued to the crews. With eighteen ships captured, the crews were looking at a large reward – if only they could save them from sinking in the storm!

Many of the ships, though taking relatively light casualties, were in terrible condition so first these had to be repaired and shored up, and the storm would blow for several days, making the work difficult.

Eleven ships of the Combined Fleets had escaped to Cadiz, and on October the 23rd they sortied out against the British, and they succeeded in recapturing two of the Spanish ships (*Santa Ana* and *Neptuno*). The crew of the *Bucentaure* overpowered the British prize crew onboard, retaking her, as did the crew of the *Algésiras*, and the crew of the *Aigle* cut the British tow ropes, though the ship foundered in the storm.

The last action that needs to be considered as part of Trafalgar was on November 4th, thirteen days after the battle, when four ships-of-the-line and four frigates took on the four French ships *Formidable*, *Scipion*, *Duguay-Troin*, and *Mont Blanc*.

When you see statistics for the Battle of Trafalgar, you will come across varying ship numbers captured, this is because some take into account just the battle, some include the storm, and some include the action of the 4th of November.

The final reckoning of the thirty-three ships in the Combined Fleets is fifteen ships lost (through explosion, burning, scuttling, and wrecked by the storm), ten captured, and eight escaped. The British losses were 458 men killed, with 1,208 injured, whilst the Combined Fleets had over 4,000 killed, over 2,500 wounded, and over 7,000 captured.

It was a remarkable victory, and the French and Spanish navies never put to sea in force again during the Napoleonic Wars, which ended in 1815. The reason for the British success is often given as the skill of the gunners, and the rate of fire they could achieve, and Nelson's tactics, but they are not the only reasons:

> The French Navy had lost a lot of its experienced officers during the French Revolution, with them having met Madam Guillotine as many had aristocratic titles and connections (hence Villeneuve dropping the 'de' from his name).

> Napoleon had taken some of the most experienced naval gunners from the fleets to help train and man his Grande Armée.

> All of the British guns by Trafalgar were fitted with gunlocks, a reliable flintlock mechanism, rather than using a linstock (slow match) to ignite the fuse.

> The French and Spanish commanders were often at loggerheads, whereas Nelson had given instructions to his Captains before the battle telling them exactly what to do if they received no new instructions.

> Cadiz had not been ready to accept the Combined Fleets to re-supply and repair them when they arrived in July, whereas the British ships had mastered the art of replenishment at sea.

Regardless of the arguments for and against, this was one of the Royal Navy's finest moments – they succeeded in eliminating the threat of invasion from Napoleon and took firm control of the seas around the island nation and beyond.

Nelson's Funeral Carriage. Courtesy of the Rijksmuseum RP-P-OB-66.570

Changing Spaces

The cockpit of HMS *Victory*, where Nelson died, has been changed many times over the years. The knee against which Nelson lay was marked with the laurel wreath in the 19th Century. When *Victory* was rammed by HMS *Neptune* in 1903, the knee was moved slightly forward, then in the 1960's moved back (see the pictures below). In 1928, when *Victory's* restoration in dry-dock was being completed, the British Sailor's Society presented a knee to HMS *Victory* which they believed had been the actual knee, given to them by King Edward VII in 1904 for their 'Nelson Room'. There was speculation that this knee was taken from the ship when damage in the area was being repaired in 1903.

Artists Impression, c1906. Note the very high deckhead: Hardy was 6 foot 4", yet in reality the orlop is lower than 5 foot in places!

The Cockpit, circa 1876

No. 6.—WHERE HE DIED.
Souvenir of HMS Victory, 1891

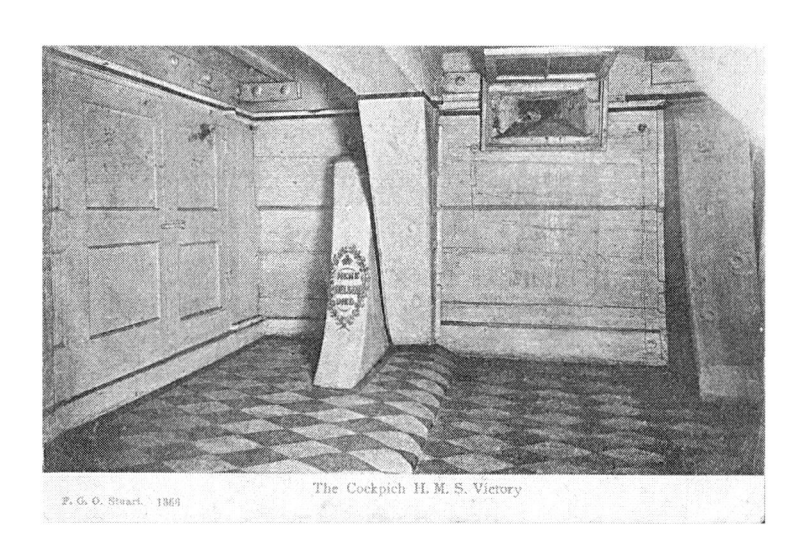

The Cockpit. The postcard is dated 1909 but the photo used in it is older.

65

In the Cockpit of HMS Victory, circa 1905

A NELSON RELIC RESTORED TO H.M.S. VICTORY.
Admiral Brock, the Commander-in-Chief, Portsmouth, receiving the knee against which Nelson was reclining when he died, on board Victory. It has been restored to the famous old ship by the British Sailors' Society. The knee will be placed in its proper position in the cockpit.

A second knee on which Nelson may have died was restored to the ship in 1928.

WHERE NELSON DIED. H.M.S. VICTORY

The Cockpit, circa 1930 (note the position of the knee)

67

The cockpit, 2023 (note the position of the knee)

The cockpit, 2024, looking forwards towards the cable tier.

The area Beatty performed his surgery on HMS Victory (2002).

A Surgeon's Toolkit

They say a workman is only as good as his tools, and for a naval surgeon of the era he would have to buy his own. And when you put yourself up for examination to pass as a surgeon, your tools would be inspected too.

In 1540, Henry VIII (*right*) combined the Guild of Surgeons (founded in the 14th Century) with the Worshipful Company of Barbers (founded in 1642) to form the Company of Barber-Surgeons. The red-and-white striped barber pole was their symbol, with the red indicating the surgery aspect and the white the barbering aspect, and they had rules laid down. If you were a barber, you could not perform surgery, and if you were a surgeon, you could not cut hair, but on a plus-note for the local populace both could extract rotten teeth.

Over the next two-hundred years, the skills and knowledge required for surgery increased, and the increasingly fractious relationship between the two ended in a break-up in 1745, with the surgeons forming the Company of Surgeons. In 1800, they are granted a Royal Charter, thus becoming the Royal College of Surgeons in London.

From the late 1700's onwards, once the surgeon, his tools, and his medicines had been inspected, the surgeon's chest would be sealed and taken onboard the ship the surgeon was destined for. As the pay was still low for a surgeon, this was to ensure they did not sell half of their supplies immediately after the inspection to improve their finances. Although the Royal Charter allowed them to still do this in 1800, it is believed that this practice had either died out by then or was fading away.

We have a comprehensive list from 1812 of what was expected to be in a surgeon's chest, and as well as general wounds, amputations, and dentistry, you may be surprised at some of the other eventualities catered for.

Starting with amputation, there would be two amputation knives, an amputation saw and a metacarpal saw (both with spare blades), two catlins (long double-bladed knives), artery forceps, two-dozen curved needles, 2 tenaculums (forceps), 6 Petit's screw tourniquets (invented by Jean Louis Petit, 1674–1750), and a pair of bone nippers (think wire cutters, but for bone).

For general surgery, there would be a pair of probe scissors, a bistoury (scalpel), probes, bullet forceps, a bullet scoop, six scalpels, a razor, two probangs (thin rods with an expanding sponge/cloth at the end for clearing the throat), ligature thread, and needles.

For trephination (drilling through the skull to relieve pressure), three trephines (circular saws), forceps, rugines (rasps/files), an elevator (to pivot the sawn-out skull piece out of the hole), and a brush.

For bleeding and cupping, six lancets, cupping equipment, and two seton needles (like a fine bradawl).

For dentistry, a dental key (if you are squeamish about dentists now, these are horrific), a gum lancet, two pairs of dental forceps, and a punch (not too dissimilar from a hole punch tool).

Finally, we have catheters, syringes, leg splints, apparatus for restoring suspended animation (bellows and associated equipment), bandages, and cloth for tourniquets.

And finally, a nice sturdy chest to organise and store everything.

Having had to buy all this equipment, not including the medicines (see next section) no wonder there was a temptation for a young surgeon starting out to sell some of his equipment after the inspection.

A Surgeon's Medicines

As well as tools, a surgeon needed a well-stocked medicine chest, and despite the common myths it wasn't all arsenic, mercury, and opium. All of the below were in the lists of William Turnbull in 1806, and were sourced from around the world.

Ammoniacum – used as a stimulant and an anti-spasmodic. It is a gum-resin derived from the Ferula genus of herbs commonly found in Libya, Egypt, Iran, and Morocco.

Calomel – mercurous chloride used as a bowel cleanser and is a mineral.

Camphor – used as a treatment to ease skin complaints. It is extracted from the wood of the camphor laurel of East Asia and the kapur tree of South-East Asia.

Emetie Tartar – a mix of calomel and antimony used to purge a stomach in both directions. Antimony is an element and Pliny the Elder mentions using it in 77 AD.

Extract of Hemlock – used as a sedative and comes from the hemlock plant (Conium maculatum) originally found in Europe and North America (though it has spread widely now).

Flowers of Zinc – Zinc oxide, used as an antiseptic and an astringent. There are records of the use of zinc oxide certainly from the 1st Century AD, if not earlier.

Gentian – used to ease digestion problems. It comes from the Gentiana genus of plants and is still used in tonics and bitters today.

Ipecacuanha – used in small doses to ease coughs, in higher doses to make you vomit. It is a plant native to Colombia, Panama, Brazil, and Costa Rica.

Laudanum – used as a painkiller and sleep aid. Only small amounts would be carried of this and, unlike today, would not be given to someone who is dying to ease their passage. It is a tincture of opium, obtained from the seed capsules of the opium poppy (Papaver somniferum).

Nitre – used for helping to break fevers and colds. It is the mineral form of potassium nitrate and is often found in cave deposits, such as old guano piles (bat or seabird excrement).

Opium – used for pain relief and extracted from the opium poppy.

Peruvian Bark – used to treat malaria and also knows as Jesuit's bark, which comes from Cinchona family of plants and contains quinine. Spanish missionaries in Peru in the 1620's were educated in the healing power of the bark by the indigenous population.

Purging Salts – used as laxatives.

Quassia – used to purge the stomach, and effective against worms, it is a plant commonly found in South America.

Salt of Steel – used to treat consumption. It is made by mixing iron filings with vitriolic acid (sulphuric acid). Once filtered, it crystalises as the liquid evaporates, leaving the '*salt*'.

Salt of Wormwood – Potassium carbonate, used to treat jaundice and liver problems, and urinary tract infections.

Senna leaves – used as a laxative.

Spirit of Mindererus – a solution of ammonium acetate, used to treat fevers.

The medicine chest onboard HMS Victory, courtesy of the National Museum of the Royal Navy, Portsmouth.

Treatments

The following extracts are from William Turnbull's 1806 book *'The Naval Surgeon Comprising the Entire Duties of professional Men at Sea'*.

Scurvy

The first appearances of this malady are marked by a languid, torpid state of body; the patient has a pale bloated look; there prevails a dejection of mind; and the breathing is affected on the slightest exertion. In a short time the gums acquire a softness and swelling; blood exudes from them, and putrid ulcers are formed. The teeth also become loose, the breath fetid, and the urine highly coloured. The heart is subject to palpitation. Oedema, or dropsical swellings, attack the lower extremities; the body is affected with wandering erratic pains of a pleuritic or rheumatic kind; and blotches and ulcers, which terminate in mortification, break out in different parts of the skin.

By the aggravation of all these symptoms, the last stage of the disease subjects the unhappy patient to the most deplorable sufferings. Excruciating pains attack the bones. The joints swell, and the tendons become rigid, preventing all motion. The fatal termination, though gradual with some, is in general sudden, especially on any attempt to move the patient, or expose him to free air.

The principles of its cure are now fully understood, and as it arises from a vitiated or scanty diet, connected with a want of that principle which vegetables supply, the means of recovery are clear, and easily applied. Indeed, whatever opinion we may form of this malady, it is an established fact, that recent vegetable matter imparts a something to the body which fortifies it against its attack; and the quantity of this something which vegetable matter supplies, in proportion to the power of the external causes favouring the disease, will, sooner or later remove the morbid symptoms.

Gonorrhoea

The leading symptom of this affection is the discharge. It is at first of a thin consistence, and of a yellow greenish colour, but as the disease advances, either from the subsiding of the inflammation, or the use of remedies producing the same effect, it acquires a more bland, white, and ropy appearance. Then the inflammation is violent, it is often tinged with blood; and, in general, from the appearance of the discharge, we are able to judge the state of the disease. Corresponding with this variety in the colour of the matter, are the other attendant symptoms of the malady. At first there prevails merely a swelling, fullness, and tightness of the parts. These are succeeded by a sensation of heat, irritation, and an acute scalding pain on the discharge of urine, which is particularly severe when the last drops are forced away. Along with these, painful spasms of the member take place, which becomes tense and rigid through its whole extent, producing erections of a most disagreeable nature. At times the whole of the lower belly becomes affected, and both the bladder and testicles are brought into a most painful and irritable state. The continuance of these symptoms varies in different cases. From ten days to a month or longer, may be considered the usual period of their duration.

...the three leading symptoms that merit attentions are the discharge, the chordee or spasms, and the occasional haemorrhage.

For the first of these symptoms the use of injections is necessary. These injections should be composed at first of substances of an oily or mucilaginous nature. As the inflammatory symptoms abate, these should be succeeded by others of an astringent and sedative kind; and their effects should be assisted by an attention to an open state of the bowels, and a proper regulation of diet. This plan is to be strictly pursued till the total disappearance of the discharge takes place.

When the chordee or spasms, the second symptom, are violent, which chiefly occurs in the night-time, the internal use of opium will be required, sometimes topical bleeding, and also the external use of antispasmodics.

Haemorrhage, the third symptom detailed, is not so frequent as the two former, and is chiefly to be removed by rest, cold, and astringents. If these to not succeed, mechanical means may be had recourse to, as the application of a bougie, or hollow catheter, or even the forming of a pressure externally.

Sea-Sickness

This complaint consists chiefly of a convulsive affection of the stomach. It is attended with great nausea and vomiting, and is occasioned by the irregular motion of the vessel. With very few exceptions, it attacks all seamen on their first voyage; and the degree of it is generally proportioned to the size of the vessel, it being most violent where the vessel is small, and least so in large vessels, on which the waves make but a slight impression. Some persons, however, are more liable to suffer from this inconvenience than others. Those in the prime of life, and of a fair complexion, have been remarked to be most susceptible of its attacks, while old persons, and those of dark habits, are least subjected to it.

The symptoms which attend this ailment are head-ache, slight fever, intense thirst, a quick pulse, and the rejection of every thing, whether solid or liquid, received into the stomach.

Though time is perhaps the only cure, various remedies have been directed to alleviate this complaint. One of the simplest is a draught or two of sea water, which, by clearing the first passages, gives effectual relief. A tea-spoon full of aether in a glass of water, will be equally efficacious. The little food taken at a time, should be eaten cold, and highly seasoned. The drink should be in sparing quantity, and well acidulated with citric acid: the clothing should be warm; and the deck be kept as much as possible by the patient, till this uneasy feeling be removed. It is constantly aggravated by indolence and inactivity, and the same effect is perceived to result from uneasiness or depression of mind.

Intoxication

Intoxication is a frequent evil amongst seamen; and the consequences to which it leads, render it a proper subject of medical investigation. It proves frequently fatal at once, or else induces fever which is equally mortal in its effects, and especially when it prevails in a warm climate. Many circumstances give a propensity to this indulgence at sea. The men in general embrace at an early period this course of life, without judgement to direct them in the line of conduct they ought to pursue. The habit of grog drinking, is a practice they immediately acquire, and the use of spirits, when they can be procured, gives them a temporary alleviation from the effects which the cold and moisture to which they are exposed produce. Their feelings being thus relieved, this indulgence becomes a confirmed habit. The propensity to it is farther favoured by that hilarity, to which they are strongly incited by the hardships they have undergone; when they joyful occasion presents itself, they sacrifice what they have dearly earned; and as the mirthful honour is always accompanied by excessive drinking, this, independently of other debaucheries, proves the after source of disease.

The treatment of intoxication is one of the most frequent duties of a Navy Surgeon; and demands immediate relief. In the fit of stupefaction, it is but too usual for the person to lie in a horizontal position, or, what is much worse, with his head hanging down. This posture ought to be altered, and the head and shoulders kept erect. The place ought to be freely ventilated, and cool, the neckcloth and collar of the shirt unbound. No persons, except those who are to give assistance, should be allowed to crowd around the patient. The next step is, to provoke vomiting by the most expeditious means, such as tickling the throat with a feather, or the finger. If raw spirit has been the inebriating liquor, and the patient still retains the powers of swallowing, he should be made to drink plentifully of water, either warm or cold, and the tickling of the throat should then be renewed, to excite the vomiting; a measure not to be given up, till the whole of the contents of the stomach are discharged. When the bloated countenance, and stertorous breathing, indicate danger of apoplexy, other means must be also had recourse to, particularly blood-letting from the temporal artery, from the jugular vein, or even from the arm, by a large orifice. But this remedy requires some caution, on account of the degree of collapse or debility that is apt to succeed. Cold applications will also be useful to the head itself, as clothes wrung out of cold vinegar and water, often renewed. Snow and ice, if at hand, are also good applications for the same purpose: but the unloading of the stomach is in all cases the quickest remedy.

Typhus

To the first symptoms described, soon succeed an exacerbation of the febrile heat, and of the state of the pulse, joined with strong marks of determination to the head. Thus the skin acquires a dry and parched feel, the tongue, hitherto not much changed, becomes hard and furred, and the secretion of the saliva as it were suspended. The confusion of head, and tendency to stupor, increase accompanied with more or less delirium, which, being at first transient, becomes gradually more continued. The state of the bowels and urine is irregular, but as the disease proceeds, diarrhoea comes on. Symptoms of putrescence now make their appearance, consisting in small livid spots, like flea-bites, dispersed over the skin. The stupor of head becomes now permanent; great anxiety prevails about the precordia; and frequent sighing takes place: haemorrhage also arises from different parts, especially from the gums and intestines, being in the latter conjoined with diarrhoea and hiccup soon succeeds, to terminate the scene.

In the early stage of this fever, as well as in every other, the first step is to cleanse the stomach and bowels, which is useful in two points of view: first, as it unloads the primae viae of any noxious contents which may second the action of the morbid cause; and, secondly, by its stimulus, opening the different excretories, which certainly display a degree of weakened power in expelling their discharges. For this purpose antimonials have generally been the favourite remedy, given either in the form of the antimonial solution, or powder, or else James's powder, which is well imitated by rubbing the tartarised antimony with magnesia or chalk. After full vomiting, in the first instance, the antimonial should be continued in smaller doses, and during its use, the patient should either lie in bed, or be kept moderately warm, and drink of thin diluent liquors; by this method the medicine will be less liable to act on the stomach and bowels. But it may be observed, that it is only in this early stage of the fever that antimonials are really useful.

When the second stage is commenced, as remarked by the degree of stupor, recourse must then be had to other remedies; and the great point is to support the strength for a certain period, both by diet and medicine.

The chief remedy with this view is wine, in liberal quantity, suited to the circumstances of the case, but given in small doses at once, and judiciously repeated. Along with this, a nourishing diet is to be administered, in the most soluble form, and such as is most grateful to the patient. By this general plan a cure will, for the most part, be effected; but in the progress of the disease particularly morbid symptoms will also require especial treatment. Thus affection of the head and difficult respiration will be relived by blisters; diarrhoea by opiates and astringents; and watchfulness and irritability by antispasmodics.

In this fever, the bark has been highly recommended by some authors, but its operation is clearly analogous to wine, and as it is apt to disagree with the stomach in the irritable state of fever, and even bring on diarrhoea, it will not be found so beneficial as this domestic article.

Yellow Fever

The most dangerous of the West India fevers, is what has been so universally known by the name of the Yellow Fever. The attack of this fever is, for the most part, sudden, and without any previous complaint on the part of the patient. The first symptoms are sudden giddiness and loss of sight, to such a degree as to make the person fall down almost insensible, in which state he will remain for half an hour or upwards. The body is overspread with a cold sweat, soon succeeded by intense heat, with a quick, small, and hard pulse. Along with this, great headache prevails, particularly affecting the fore and hinder parts. This is accompanied by pain at the right side, and much oppression at the precordia. In this fever the eyes are much inflamed and watery, protruding and rolling in a wild manner. The face is greatly flushed; and a strong determination to the head in general prevails. With these primary symptoms are connected much heat of stomach, and strong tendency to bilious vomitings. Violent pain is also felt in the small of the back and calves and legs.

...The first of these, after evacuating in the usual manner of the stomach and bowels, by the antimonial solution, consists of throwing in the bark and acids, with the addition of wine, in such quantities as the stomach will bear; and as the irritability of this viscus is here very great, an occasional opiate will be necessary; or, if this does not succeed, the bark must be exhibited in the form of clysters. Of the acids, the vegetable is to be preferred and all drinks given the patient should consist of a proportion of it.

During this general treatment, particular symptoms will require attentions. Thus, pain and increased discharge will call for the interposition of opiates, which should be administered in small doses, in order to be retained; and costiveness, if it prevail, must be removed by acescent laxatives. During this course, a free exposure of the patient to a dry cool air is to be recommended.

Small-pox

Small-pox is a disease which very often appears at sea; and is also frequently fatal. The infection is conveyed by the intercourse with the shore; seaman brought up in merchant services generally go to sea very young, and when they continue on long voyages, they often avoid entirely the contagion of small-pox till they grow up to manhood, when being brought into his Majesty's service, and placed aboard a sip of war, they are apt to catch the disease in the manner pointed out.

The frequency of this malady in the fleet, induced Dr. Trotter to propose a general inoculation[118]; and the success attending this practice, in the ships in which it was attempted, justified the propriety of the measure. In suggesting it, however, Dr. Trotter found it difficult to combat the scruples of the seamen, arising from religious prejudices; but since that time inoculation has been regularly performed, both with variolous matter, and more recently, with the cow-pox, a substitute possessing still greater advantages. As the subject is now so well understood, and the prejudices of the crew done away, it is unnecessary to enter farther into the subject.

---

[118] **Thomas Trotter (1760-1832). In 1800 the Sick and Hurt Board approved the proposal to inoculate both sufferers and those who had never had smallpox.**

Scorches

Scorches from gunpowder are equally frequent with gun-shot wounds. They arise from powder accidentally exploding in an engagement; and these accidents are very frequent and fatal. The treatment here is the same as in other cases of burns. The best applications are found to be lintseed-oil, mixed with lime-water or cerussa. This treatment must be joined with the use of opium and laxatives, according to circumstances.

Amputation

... in order to save the life of the patient, its removal becomes the expedient left, and amputation must accordingly be performed. The improved state of surgery has rendered this a successful operation, as well at the great joints of the shoulder and the thigh, as in the course of the extremities. The great point at sea, in amputation, is to restrain the hemorrhage in the first instance, so that there may be no occasion afterwards to disturb the patient, or interrupt the cure by any accident of hemorrhage, a circumstance which is so apt to occur, from the scorbutic state of the fluids. Too much attention, therefore, cannot be paid to take up every vessel, however small, that presents itself; and on the time spent in this part of the operation much of its success will depend. Another circumstance no less important, is making the flap so large as to heal by the first intention. If these two rules are kept in view, the success of amputation at sea will be equally great as in the hospital. As this operation is more frequent on ship-board than any other, the circumstances attending it should be more closely studied by the Naval Surgeon than most operations; at the same time, it may be remarked, that it is attended by a greater fatality than any other part of the business of surgery, as the inspection of the Naval Journals will shew.

The steps of the operation itself may be simply reduced to four leading ones. The first is the prevent of hemorrhage, which is done by a full command of the tourniquet in the first instance, and a minute application of the tenaculum afterwards, for the reasons just now assigned. The second important step in the operation, is the separation of the nerves from the other parts, which should take place as completely as the time will permit, in order to prevent the symptoms of pain and spasm, which are so unfavourable to the cure. The third important step, already noticed, is the proportion of the stump, which should be no more than completely to cover the denuded parts, and not so much as to lap over and endanger the formation of matter. The last circumstance regards the after treatment; and here the great object so to obviate inflammation in the first instance, and afterwards to check any excess of discharge, which might reduce the constitution of the patient.

Drowning

In closing the account of Occasional Accidents at Sea, drowning must not be omitted, it being one which too frequently occurs. The symptoms which here mark the progress to death are as follows: the circulation becomes first more feeble and slow, and an anxiety is next felt about the praecordia, which the drowning person attempts to relieve by his rising to the surface of the water, if it be in his power. He then discharges a quantity of air from his lungs, in place of which water is received; the oppression of the chest increases; and he still continues to expel air, and to take in water in return.

...The means of restoring animation, where this accident is early noticed, are numerous, and in no situation, however desperate, should they be omitted. They consist chiefly in the proper application of heat, and the irritation of some of the vital organs, particularly the brain, lungs, and primae viae.

The heat is to be applied in a gradual degree. The body, having been placed in a horizontal posture on a bed, or in another situation, is to be covered with warm dry cloths, occasionally renewed. A warm night-cap is to be put on the head, and bags of warm sand placed at the feet. Even friction may be conjoined with this application of heat; and the rubbing of the body with warm dry flannels at the same time, will have much influence. The heat must be gradually increased as the symptoms of animation return. Next to the application of heat, the re-establishment of respiration is an important step. The lungs should be immediately inflated, by inserting a pipe in one nostril, compressing the other, and shutting the mouth, when a person applying his mouth to the pipe, and blowing through it, will inflate the lungs. When these means seem to have some effect, volatile applications to the nostrils, temples, etc. to stimulate the brain, may next be attempted; besides which, irritation of the stomach, by vomits and other stimulants, has been employed; and also that of the intestines, by the injection of fumes of tobacco.

Navy Bites Volume 1 contains thirty-two tales from the Royal Navy, covering the great, the bizarre, and the tragic. Spanning from 1546 — when the Royal Navy was formed — through to 1993, this book brings to life the events that have shaped the RN. Whether it be the invasion of the Isle of Wight, women disguising themselves as men to serve, stone frigates, ships of ice and sawdust, the longest row, flat-pack ships, bizarre camouflage, the odd re-use of damaged ships, the Gibraltar apes, or nuclear London; this book covers them all.

Things to See

Kensal Green Cemetery, London

William Beatty is buried in Kensal Green, and though originally in an unmarked vault, in 1995 the 1805 Club erected a memorial outside the vault to him.

Beatty's Medicine Chest, St. Luke's Church, Haslar, Gosport

Bought by crowd-funding to stop it from being exported, Beatty's medicine chest, dating from 1803, is now on display at St. Luke's Church in Gosport.

Beatty's Surgical Tool Chest, Royal College of Physicians and Surgeons of Glasgow

A chest containing several of Beatty's tools, including an amputation knife, tourniquet, bullet forceps and a bow saw.

The Musket-ball That Killed Nelson, Windsor Castle

Beatty extracted the musket-ball that killed Nelson during the autopsy, and on Beatty's death was gifted by his family to Queen Victoria in 1842. It is deformed where it went through the body, and you can see threads of gold-braid embedded.

Nelson's Uniform, National Maritime Museum, Greenwich

The uniform Nelson was wearing when he was shot, along with his blood-stained stockings (though it is the blood of John Scott, not Nelson).

HMS *Victory*, Portsmouth Historic Dockyard

See the ultimate in Georgian engineering, the first-rate ship-of-the-line HMS *Victory*, on which Nelson died and Beatty served.

Nelson's Column, Trafalgar Square

London. Nelson's Column, Trafalgar Square, Oct. 21, 1905.
Centenary Battle of Trafalgar

83

Further Reading and Resources

To list all of the books written on Nelson and the Battle of Trafalgar would take a volume in its own right, so here I have listed some of the key medical accounts from the period covering the medical aspects and those of life at sea.

Nelson's Surgeon: William Beatty, Naval Medicine, and the Battle of Trafalgar (LWB Brockliss, Cardwell, and Moss)

A biography of William Beatty, following his career as a naval surgeon and then as he progresses into a wealthy man with varied business interests.

Naval Surgeon: Life and Death at Sea in the Age of Sail (J. Worth Estes)

For nearly two years, Peter St. Medard was the surgeon onboard the American frigate, *New York*, from 1802. This book takes his detailed notes of the time and adds in personal correspondence and a lot of research.

Fiddlers and Whores: The Candid Memoirs of a Surgeon in Nelson's Fleet (James Lowry)

These are the memoirs of a young Irish surgeon between 1797 and 1804. Though light on medical details, he does give his impressions as he travels through various ports and cities. Be warned though, his views on other cultures are very dismissive and bigoted.

The Naval Surgeon Comprising the Entire Duties of Professional Men at Sea (William Turnbull)

At the other end of the scale, from 1806, we have this tome, which is everything a surgeon needed to know. Descriptions of diseases for each of the stations (Channel, West India, East India, Africa) and their treatments, how to treat gunshot wounds, what diet men should eat, attention to hammocks and clothing, exercise, ulcers, hernias, sexually transmitted diseases, drowning, amputation, and the medicines to be carried.

Outlines of Naval Surgery (John Wilson)

This volume from 1846 is similar to the above book but shows you the advances in medicines and procedures in the forty years that have passed.

Rough Medicine: Surgeons at Sea in the Age of Sail (Joan Druett)

This book takes us through events in the lives of various surgeons from the early 1600's to the 1830's. It is well researched and has some great tales in it.

Naval Surgeon: The Voyages of Dr. Edward H. Cree (Edward H. Cree)

These are the personal log entries of the author between 1837 and 1856, during which he travels out to China, before heading out for the Crimean War.

Scurvy (Jonathan Lamb)

This traces the effect that scurvy had on various seafaring nations during Eighteenth Century.

The Age of Scurvy: How A Surgeon, A Mariner And A Gentleman Helped Britain Win The Battle Of Trafalgar (Stephen R. Brown)

This book follows George Anson, James Lind, James Cook, and Gilbert Blane as they struggle with the effects of scurvy and look to find a way to fight its effects.

Surgeons of the Fleet: The Royal Navy and Its Medics from Trafalgar to Jutland (David McLean)

This book takes you through naval medicine and its transformation from Trafalgar through to the First World War, especially focussing on the reforms in the administration, recruitment, and training of medical staff.

Societies and Organisations

The National Museum of the Royal Navy, Portsmouth – the trustees of HMS *Victory* and her legacy, and a superb naval museum.

The National Maritime Museum, Greenwich – one of the best maritime museums in the UK.

The Society for Nautical Research – the world's leading society for maritime history.

The 1805 Club – through their programme of initiatives, publications, research and education, are building a global community open to enthusiasts of naval history from all backgrounds. Recognising the role of the world's sailing navies of the Georgian period (1714-1837) and promoting their legacy into the modern seafaring age, they also preserve Georgian naval monuments.

The Trafalgar Way – dedicated to commemorating the race from Falmouth to London to bring back the first news from the Battle of Trafalgar.

The Naval Dockyards Society - promoting research into the history of naval dockyards, and their associated skills and practices, around the world.

The Trafalgar Times – A quarterly newsletter aimed at all things Age of Sail, including book reviews, museum news, and much more.

Further Online Resources

History Hit TV – An online History channel with podcasts and films covering a huge range of historical topics.

The Mariner's Mirror Podcast – A regular podcast from the Society for Nautical Research.

Nelson's Pillar in Dublin, 1941 (destroyed in 1966), Rijksmueum, RP-P-2018-2027

A Drop of Nelson's Blood

It has long been rumoured that the sailors were drinking the brandy from the barrel that contained Nelson's body on the voyage from Cape Trafalgar to Gibraltar. To be clear, there are no primary sources to support this – the level of the brandy would have gone down through absorption by the body and evaporation. It did, however, give rise to the phrase *'tapping the Admiral'*. Although Nelson was pickled in brandy, 'Nelson's Blood' refers to rum.

Well, a drop of Nelson's blood wouldn't do us any harm
And a drop of Nelson's blood wouldn't do us any harm
And a drop of Nelson's blood wouldn't do us any harm
And we'll all hang on behind

Come on and roll the old chariot along
(Yes, we'll) roll the old chariot along
(Come on and) roll the old chariot along
And we'll all hang on behind

And a damn good floggin' wouldn't do us any harm
And a damn good floggin' wouldn't do us any harm
And a damn good floggin' wouldn't do us any harm
And we'll all hang on behind

Come on and roll the old chariot along
(Yes, we'll) roll the old chariot along
(Come on and) roll the old chariot along
And we'll all hang on behind

And a nice fat cook wouldn't do us any harm
And a nice fat cook wouldn't do us any harm
And a nice fat cook wouldn't do us any harm
And we'll all hang on behind

Come on and roll the old chariot along
(Yes, we'll) roll the old chariot along
(Come on and) roll the old chariot along
And we'll all hang on behind

And a night with the girls wouldn't do us any harm
And a night with the girls wouldn't do us any harm
And a night with the girls wouldn't do us any harm
And we'll all hang on behind

Come on and roll the old chariot along
(Yes, we'll) roll the old chariot along
(Come on and) roll the old chariot along
And we'll all hang on behind

And a roll in the clover wouldn't do us any harm
And a roll in the clover wouldn't do us any harm
And a roll in the clover wouldn't do us any harm
And we'll all hang on behind

Come on and roll the old chariot along
(Yes, we'll) roll the old chariot along
(Come on and) roll the old chariot along
And we'll all hang on behind

Well, a drop of Nelson's blood wouldn't do us any harm
And a drop of Nelson's blood wouldn't do us any harm
And a drop of Nelson's blood wouldn't do us any harm
And we'll all hang on behind

Come on and roll the old chariot along
(Yes, we'll) roll the old chariot along
(Come on and) roll the old chariot along
And we'll all hang on behind

There are different versions of the lyrics available, *'another month's pay'*, *'a night with the fiddler'*, *'a tight-waisted girl'*, *'we'll be all right if we make it round the horn'*. The version you hear/sing will probably depend on the expected sensibilities around you, but it is a great shanty for tailoring the lyrics.

The Bitesize Military History Quiz Book tests your knowledge and your wits against crosswords and puzzles all themed around military history.
Do you know your operations of World War II? Your ships from the Battle of Trafalgar? Your British castles? Famous Admirals? The English Civil War? The American Civil War? When the Spitfire came into service? How many crew were in a Halifax bomber? The Roman World?
All these and more are covered in this book.

The award-winning Mariner's Mirror Podcast is the world's no.1 podcast dedicated to all of maritime and naval history. Presented by Dr Sam Willis the podcast has been downloaded and viewed by millions, worldwide. With regular interviews and constant innovative video content the Mariner's Mirror podcast will change the way that you think about the world's maritime past. It is published in association with the Society for Nautical Research and the Lloyd's Register Foundation.

The second in the Navy Notes series, Jack Nastyface takes you onboard HMS Revenge, from the Battle of Trafalgar to the Walcheren Campaign. Written by William Robinson, and published in 1836, this account has been annotated, indexed, and contains supplementary material.

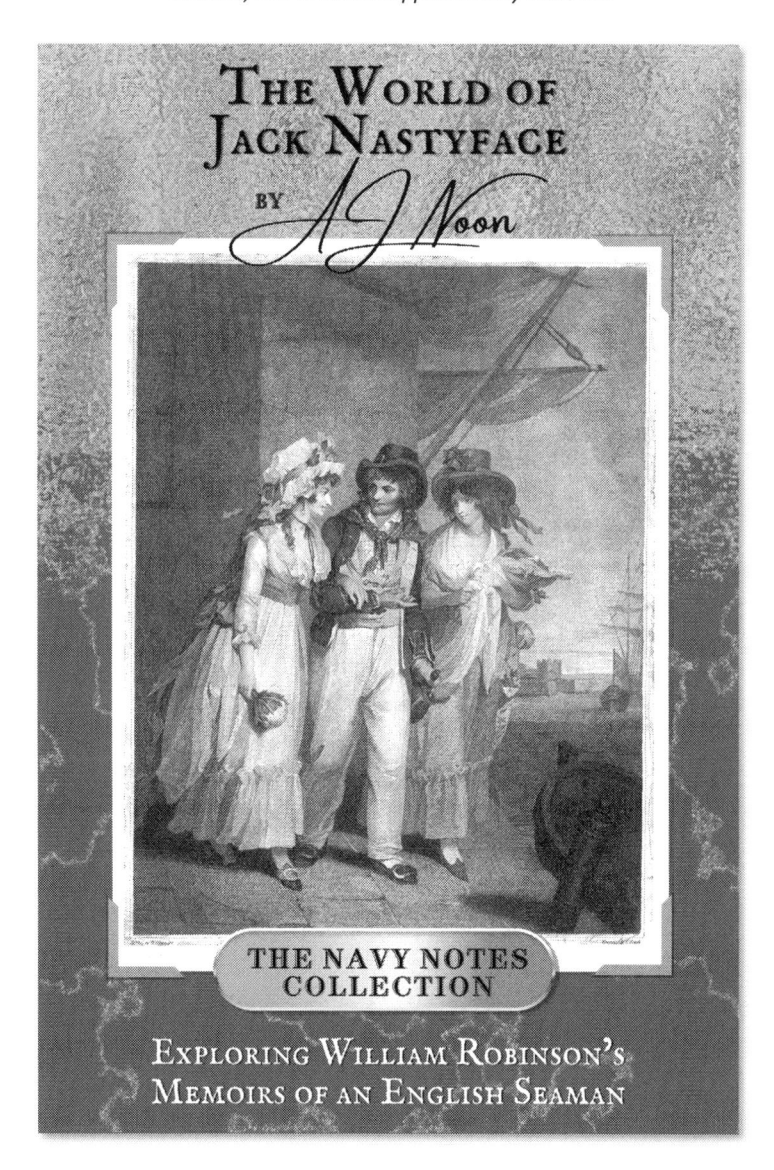

THE WORLD OF JACK NASTYFACE

BY A J Noon

THE NAVY NOTES COLLECTION

EXPLORING WILLIAM ROBINSON'S MEMOIRS OF AN ENGLISH SEAMAN

Index

1805 Club, the, 82
Aboukir Bay, 7, 8, 38
Adair, William, 28, 39, 41
Admiralty, the, 48
Affleck, Thomas, 8
Aide-de-camp, 34
Aigle, 62
Alderney, 8
Algésiras, 62
Algiers, 58
ammoniacum, 71
amputation, 8, 52, 70, 79
anchor, 17, 27, 36
Antigua, 11
artery, 53
assistant surgeons, 33, 34
Atkinson, Thomas, 29
Austria, 18
Barbados, 11
Barbary, 44
barber pole, 69
barometer, 52
Battle
  of Cape Finisterre, 18
  of Copenhagen, 21
  of the Nile, 8, 21, 38, 48
  of Trafalgar, 8, 38, 50, 62
Baudoin, Louis Alexis, 29
Bay of Biscay, 16
Bayntun, Henry William, 26
Berry, Edward, 18
Bickerton, Richard, 16
Blackwood, Henry, 20, 23, 26, 57, 59
Bligh, George, 39
blockade, 11
boats, 26
Bonaparte, Napoleon, 9
brandy, 42, 43, 44, 47, 48, 87
Bristol, 51
British Sailor's Society, the, 64
Browne, George, 30
Bucentaure, 24, 29, 62
Buckler's Hard,, 20
Bulkley, Richard, 34
Burke, Walter, 31, 33, 34, 35, 37, 38
Burnham Thorpe, 50
Byard, Thomas, 43
Cadiz, 11, 13, 16, 17, 20, 24, 27, 54, 57, 58, 59, 62, 63
Calais, 21
Calder, Robert, 13, 18
calomel, 71

camphor, 47, 71
Cape
  Finisterre, 13
  François, 21
  Spartel, 59
  St. Mary's, 17
  St. Vincent, 8, 16, 17, 38
  Trafalgar, 41, 59, 87
Capel, Thomas Bladen, 23
Captain's Clerk, 31
Carolina, Maria, 23
cask, 42, 43, 44
casualties, 25, 28, 42, 44, 62
champagne, 51
Channel Fleet, physician of the, 9
chaplain, 21
Chatham, 44
Chevallier, Henry Lew, 37
Clerical, Medical and General Life Assurance Company, 9
cockpit, 31, 32, 35, 46, 64
codicil, 22
coffin, 48, 49
Collingwood
  Cuthbert, 16, 19, 21, 25, 27, 36, 38, 44, 57
  Edward, 39
Combined Fleets, 11, 13, 17, 18, 20, 22, 24, 41, 46, 58, 59, 62
Company of Barber-Surgeons, the, 69
Company of Surgeons, the, 7, 69
Copenhagen, 38
Corsica, 52
courts-martial, 8, 18
cupping, 70
Deniéport, Louis-Gabriel, 42
dentistry, 70
Devis, Arthur William, 60
diet, 51
Digby, Henry, 8
dinner, 51
domestics, 35
drowning, 80
Duff, George, 19
Duguay-Troin, 62
Duke of Wellington, 9
Dumanoir le Pelley, Pierre, 40
Dundas, Thomas, 23
Edinburgh, 9
Egypt, 11, 22, 23, 25

emetie tartar, 71
England, 43
England Expects Every Man Will Do His Duty, 26
epaulette, 45, 46, 47
exercise, 51
eye, 52
fire, 42
Firme, 13
Fitzroy, Augustus, 7
flowers of zinc, 71
foreign secretary, 21
Formidable, 62
French Revolution, the, 24, 63
frock-coat, 21
Gardoqui, Don José de, 27
General Memorandum, 54
gentian, 71
Germany, 18
Gibraltar, 13, 17, 18, 43, 44, 58, 87
Gibraltar Bay, 44
globus hystericus, 51
God, 22
gonorrhoea, 73
Gosport, 82
gout, 51
Grande Armée, 63
Gravina, Don Federico Carlos, 11
great coat, 51
Greenwich, 15
Greenwich Hospital, 9, 15, 44, 49
grenades, 39
Grey, George, 49
Guildford, 49
guillotine, 63
gunlocks, 63
Gunner, 34
Hallowell, Benjamin, 48
Hamilton
  Emma, 21, 22, 23, 32, 34, 35, 36, 37
  William, 22, 32
handkerchief, 31
Hardy
  Thomas, 18, 20, 21, 23, 25, 26, 28, 30, 34, 37, 41, 43, 44, 48, 50
Harvey, Eliab, 26
Hawksmoor, Nicholas, 15
hemlock, extract of, 71
HMS
  Africa, 18
  Agamemnon, 18, 58
  Ajax, 16, 17
  Alcmene, 8

92

Alligator, 7
Amethyst, 8
Amphion, 57, 58
Belleisle, 18, 19, 44, 58
Bellerophon, 58
Britannia, 58
Canopus, 17
Colossus, 18, 19, 58, 59
Constance, 57
Decade, 16
Defence, 18, 19, 58, 59
Defiance, 18
Dictator, 7
Diligent, 58
Donegal, 18, 58
Dreadnought, 21, 58
Entreprenante, 19
Euryalus, 16, 17, 20, 23, 26, 57
Flying Fish, 7
Foudroyant, 43
Hermione, 7
Hydra, 17, 57
Iphigenia, 7
Leviathan, 18, 26, 58
Mars, 18, 19, 58, 59
Naiad, 16, 23, 59
Neptune, 64
Orion, 58
Phoebe, 23, 59
Pickle, 57
Polyphemus, 19, 58
Pomona, 7
Prince, 58
Prince of Wales, 13, 18
Queen, 17
Resistance, 8
Retaliation, 7
Retribution, 7
Royal Sovereign, 18, 21, 25, 27, 38
Sirius, 23
Spencer, 8, 17
Sussex, 9
Swiftsure, 41
Temeraire, 26, 29, 30, 39, 40
Thunderer, 16, 17
Tigre, 17
Victory, 5, 7, 8, 15, 17, 21, 23, 24, 28, 41, 54, 60, 64, 82
Weazle, 58
Zealous, 17
Hope, George, 19
indigestion, 51
Intoxication, 75
ipecacuanha, 71
iron hoops, 19
Isle of Wight, 16, 44
Jamaica, 21

Jervis, John, 22
Kensal Green cemetery, 9, 82
King
  Edward VII, 64
  Ferdinand I, 22
  Henry VIII, 69
  of Naples, 18, 22
  of Spain, 22
King, Andrew, 30
kismet, 36
kiss, 36
La Fougueux, 29
La Redoutable, 46
L'Achille, 42
laudanum, 71
leaguer, 42
lemonade, 32, 33
Life of Lord Nelson, the, 16
Lisbon, 57
London and Greenwich Railway, 9
London Company of Surgeons, the, 7
Londonderry, 7
L'Orient, 48, 49
Louis, Thomas, 17
Lucas, Jean Jacques Etienne, 29
Lyon, Amy, 21
Mack von Leiberich, Karl, 18
Malcolm, Pulteney, 18
Martinique, 11
Master, 29
medicine chest, 71
Memorandum Book, 57
Merton Place, 50
Mont Blanc, 62
monument, 50
morass, 50
Morris, James Nicoll, 19
Mr. BEATTY, Lord NELSON is here, 31
musket-ball, 42, 45, 46, 47, 82
myrrh, 48
Naples, 8, 21
Napoleon, 9
naval hospital, 43
Navarrete, Ignacio María de Álava y, 27
Nelson
  daughter, 23
  Duke of Bronte, 23
  Horatia, 23, 32, 37
  Horatio, 15, 46
Nelson, autopsy, 45, 46, 52
Nelson, eye, 52
Nelson, Fanny, 21
Nelson, father, 50

Nelson, health, 50
Nelson, Horatio, 11
Nelson, last words, 37
Nelson, preservation of body, 42
Nelson, quote
  Kiss me, Hardy, 36
  That is well, but I bargained for twenty, 36
  They have done for me at last, HARDY, 30
  This is too warm work, 28
  Will no one bring Hardy to me?, 34
Nelson, quote
  before a fortnight the Enemy will be *at sea, the business will be done, and we shall be looking out for England*, 18
  Collingwood is doing well, 27
  Is that poor SCOTT that is gone?, 28
  Poor fellow!, 28
  Take care of my Guardian Angel, 21
  the 21st of October was the happiest day in the year among his family, 21
  This day or to-morrow will be a fortunate one for you, young men, 19
Nelson, quote
  my backbone is shot through, 30
Nelson, quote
  Doctor, I told you so. Doctor, I am gone, 32
Nelson, quote
  I felt it break my back, 32
Nelson, quote
  fan, fan, drink, drink, 33
Nelson, quote
  it is all over, 33
Nelson, quote
  Remember me to your father, 34
Nelson, quote
  Well, Hardy, how goes the battle?, 34
Nelson, quote

93

I hope none of our ships have struck, HARDY, 34
Nelson, quote
  I am a dead man, Hardy. I am going fast, 34
Nelson, quote
  all power of motion and feeling below my breast are gone, 35
Nelson, quote
  Don't throw me overboard, 36
Nelson, quote
  never forget Horatia, 37
Nelson, quote
  Thank GOD, I have done my duty, 37
Nelson, quote
  Should I be killed, Hardy, and my Country not bury me, you know what to do with me, 50
Nelson, quote
  no Captain can do very wrong if he places his ship alongside that of an Enemy, 55
Nelson, quote
  completely to annihilate the Enemy's Fleet!, 55
Nelson's Blood, A Drop Of, 87
Nelson's Column, 9
Neptuno, 62
Nisbet, Frances, 21
nitre, 71
noise, 38
Nore, the, 44
Norfolk, 50
Ogilvie, David, 27, 39
opium, 71
orlop, 31
Painted Hall, the, 15
Palmer, Alexander, 39
Pasco
  John, 27, 33
Peake, James, 35
Perle, 8
Peruvian bark, 71
Petit, Jean Louis, 70
Pierrepoint, William, 16
Plymouth, 8, 9, 16, 43
Pollard, John, 41
Portsmouth, 44, 49, 57
prayer, 22, 49
prizes, 62
promotion, 19

Prowse, William, 23
Public Secretary, 25
purging salts, 72
Purser, 31
putrefaction, 45
quassia, 72
Queen
  of Naples, 23
Quilliam, John, 39
Ram
  William, 31
  William Andrew, 31
Redoutable, 29, 30, 39, 40, 41, 42
Reeves, Lewis B, 35
reviews, 5
Rivers, William, 34
Rochefort squadron, 58
Rotely, Lewis, 41
Rotherham, Edward, 25
Royal Charter, 69
Royal College of Surgeons in London, the, 69
Royal Marines, 28, 30, 39, 41, 43
rum, 42
Rutherford, William, 41
Saint Paul's Cathedral, 50
salt of steel, 72
salt of wormwood, 72
San Rafael, 13
Santa Ana, 27, 62
Santissima Trinidada, 24, 29
Scipion, 62
scorches, 79
Scott
  Alexander John, 21, 25, 32, 33, 35, 37, 49
  John, 25, 28, 30, 82
scurvy, 51, 73
sea-sickness, 74
Secker, James, 30
senna leaves, 72
servants, 52
Sheerness, 9, 44
Sicily, 23
sick-report, 25
Siege of Calvi, 52
signal, 26, 36, 58
  England Expects Every Man Will Do His Duty, 26
  he depended on the Euryalus for keeping sight of the Enemy during the night, 20
  prepare to anchor after the close of the day, 27

  the Enemy appeared determined to go to the westward, 20
  the Enemy bearing north, 19
  the Enemy being at sea, 19
  the Enemy were coming out of port, 18
  the Enemy's Commander in Chief was in a frigate, 27
Signal Officer, 27
Small-pox, 78
Smith, Neil, 33
Smyth, George, 7
Solent, the, 44
Spain, 22
spine, 46
spirit of mindererus, 72
spirit of wine, 43, 44, 48
Spithead, 25, 44
St. Helen's, 16, 25, 57
St. Luke's Church, 82
state funeral, 50
steward, 37
Stirling, Charles, 16
stockings, 52
storm, 41, 43, 62
Strachan
  Richard, 40, 58
Straits of Gibraltar, 17, 19, 44, 58, 59
stump, 52
Suckling, Maurice, 21
surgeon, 69
surgery, 70
Sutton, Samuel, 57
sword, 21
Syracuse, 23
tactics, 63
Tagus, the, 57
tapping the Admiral, 87
Tenerife, 52
Tetuan Bay, 44
Toulon, 11
Trafalgar, 17
Trafalgar Square, 9
Treaty of Amiens, 8
trephination, 70
Trotter, Thomas, 78
Turnbull, William, 71
Typhus, 76
uniform, 21, 25, 26, 30, 45, 82
Union Jack, 27
University of Greenwich, 15
vertebræ, 46
Villeneuve, Pierre-Charles, 11, 13, 24

viscera, 52	will, 22	Worshipful Company of Barbers, the, 69
waistcoat, 52	codicil, 22	
Ward, Philip, 32	William, Westenburgh, 33	Wren, Christopher, 15
water, 51	Williams, Edward, 30	yellow fever, 7, 77
West Indies, 7, 11, 25, 35	*wind of shot*, 31	Yule, John, 30
Westminster Abbey, 50	wine, 33, 51	
Whipple, Thomas, 31	Wollward, Frances, 21	

Portrait of a midshipman, probably Admiral Nelson (1822-1845, courtesy of the Rijksmuseum RP-P-1900-A-22137

Printed in Great Britain
by Amazon

cdc8bca2-ed88-499b-a42c-eade51d89d25R01